A MANUAL
OF VENEERING

PAUL VILLIARD

DOVER PUBLICATIONS, INC.
NEW YORK

International Standard Book Number: 0-486-23217-4
Library of Congress Catalog Card Number: 75-13123

Manufactured in the United States of America
Dover Publications, Inc.
180 Varick Street
New York, N.Y. 10014

To Gertrude, Paul, and William

FOREWORD

There are still a few unenlightened souls who think one is supposed to "sneer when saying veneer." However, most people are now aware of the tremendous advantages of veneered construction. Dating from the time of the early Egyptians, this construction is now used on 90 per cent of all furniture from the most costly to the least expensive. Only veneering makes possible panels which are relatively free of dimension changes in any degree of humidity, the beautiful effect of the various types of figure matching, and furniture and other products made of the exotic and rare hardwood species of the world at prices almost anyone can afford. At one time only royalty could afford such things. The grand piano could not be constructed any other way.

As pointed out so well by the author, those readers planning to work with veneers may anticipate a tremendous thrill of satisfaction as their creations come alive with the beauty of matched hardwood veneer figure patterns. For those of you with some experience in veneering, this book will increase your skills and enable you to create more challenging projects.

The hardwood veneer industry is deeply indebted to Paul Villiard and the publisher for having put the record straight regarding veneered construction and for having opened up in such a clear and interesting fashion the methods and satisfaction of working with this marvelous material.

E. HOWARD GATEWOOD
Executive Vice President
Fine Hardwoods Association
Chicago, Illinois

PREFACE

There are many books available on the fundamentals of furniture-making, but few that deal with the methods of constructing and working the veneer itself. Any discussion of veneer is usually confined to prepared panels, which limits the craftsman to the comparatively few species of veneer used by the commercial veneering companies.

Every once in a while, a large lumber or plywood company will offer a limited number of panels of plywood faced with a really fine veneer, one seldom to be found commercially. But these occasions are uncommon and such choice items are usually snapped up at once by some furniture manufacturer. The craftsman must be constantly on the alert, always browsing through stocks of plywood suppliers in hope of finding a rare piece that has been overlooked.

The purpose of this book is to acquaint you with the wide variety of unusual woods available in sheet veneer, and to show you how to construct the plywood panel: the treatment of the veneer, gluing, matching, curing, and finishing. The actual furniture-making is left for another volume.

The satisfaction of taking your first panel of veneered work out of your own veneer press is literally indescribable. That panel is a thing of beauty, even with all the tape and surface glue! These detractions fade before the beauty of the grain and figure of the wood, and appreciation of the work that went into it. The innermost construction is now a matter of intimate knowledge, a part

ix

of your own craftsmanship. And the sight of that first panel brings to the fore your uttermost desire to improve your work, matching, selection, on subsequent panels.

I believe that veneering does more to strengthen the desire for the development of real workmanship than any other single craft. The very beauty of the veneer demands care, time, and patience in setting up the panel in order that the result do justice to the raw materials. A person may be instructed time and again to take care and spend time doing everything just so, but comparison of a veneered panel perfectly laid up with one in which the matching was off, or the edging so poorly done that an unsightly glue-line showed right down the center, is a graphic lesson in the value of tender-loving-care in working with rare woods.

There is an irreparable sense of loss in a spoiled panel, a sense of guilt in your awareness that your work was something less than the best you could do. The rare veneer can never be reclaimed. That particular piece of the hidden beauty of the world is gone forever, ruined by shoddy workmanship. There is not another like it, and probably never will be again.

Treat each sheet of veneer, then, with the reverence due an irreplaceable treasure. Give it only your very best effort in fabricating the panel from it. Meticulously check every operation before you make a final move to be certain that you are ready for the next step. If you are not sure, do it over: if there is the slightest doubt in your mind that the edge-joint is not perfect, do it over; if you think there is some tiny possibility that the pieces slipped when you taped them together before gluing, tape them over. There is nothing to your detriment in doing a job over and over until you know it is right; there is a lot against allowing yourself to let something slide by that is less than your best. The thought that it will not readily be seen or that only you will know is an unworthy one—unworthy of the beauty of the material you are working with, unworthy of the pride of craftsmanship that is every person's heritage. Whether that craftsmanship be displayed in veneering, cooking, selling automobiles, or in any activity whatsoever, anything less than your best effort is bound to show and be seen, by others but especially by yourself.

The tree from which the wonderful thin sheets of veneer came took possibly a hundred years or more to grow. If you remember that, the few extra hours you spend in being especially careful, especially cautious, will seem as nothing when that time spent may preserve a thing of beauty to be enjoyed and admired for many years—even for many generations to come.

PAUL VILLIARD

Saugerties, New York
March, 1968

LIST OF SUPPLIERS

The following is a partial listing of companies which supply veneers. All of them have catalogs which they will send on request.

Albert Constantine & Son
2050 Eastchester Rd.
Bronx, New York 10461

Woodcraft Supply Corporation
313 Montvale Ave.
Woburn, Massachusetts 01801

Frank Mittermeier Inc.
3577 East Tremont Ave.
Bronx, New York 10465

Homecraft Veneer
Box 3
Latrobe, Pennsylvania 15650

New England Craftsman
Box 20
Elnora, New York 12065

Educational Lumber Co. Inc.
Box 5373, Meadow Rd.
Asheville,
North Carolina 28803

Wood Shed
1807 Elmwood Ave.
Buffalo, New York 14207

Craftsman's Wood Service Co.
2727 South Mary St.
Chicago, Illinois 60608

Minnesota Woodworker Supply Co.
Rogers, Minnesota 55374

Real Woods
107 Trumbull St.
Elizabeth, New Jersey 07206

Robert M. Albrecht
8635 Yolanda Ave.
Northridge, California 91324

M & M Hardwood
5344 Vineland
North Hollywood,
California 91601

Gustin Wood Finishes Inc.
3630 East Tenth St.
Bloomington, Indiana 47401

ACKNOWLEDGMENTS

I would like to express my grateful appreciation to the following companies for their inestimable assistance in preparing this volume:

To the Fine Hardwoods Association for allowing me to quote from their many publications, especially "Fine Hardwoods Selectorama" and pamphlets numbered 1, 3, and 5 in the Educational Series, which contained a wealth of material that would otherwise have been difficult to obtain; and for the use of photographs of the commercial production of veneers appearing on pages 8, 9, and 12.

To the Adjustable Clamp Company for supplying me with clamps to use in illustrating techniques of veneering; and for photographs appearing on pages 27, 31, and 42.

To Albert Constantine and Son for permission to quote from their 1954 publication, *Veneering Made Easy* by Herman Hjorth, and for aid in selecting veneers and inlays for photographic purposes.

To H. L. Wild Company for supplying the veneer repair punches shown in this book.

Other publications referred to in preparing this book were:

"Characteristics of Modern Woods," published in 1956 by the Roddis Plywood Corporation, Marshfield, Wisconsin;

ACKNOWLEDGMENTS

"What Everyone Should Know About Mahogany," published in 1955 by the Mahogany Association, Inc., Chicago, Illinois; *The Practical Book of Period Furniture*, J. B. Lippincott Company, Philadelphia, Pennsylvania, 1914.

And to my friends who helped in so many ways to carry this writing through to completion, and who are too numerous to list individually, are due my special thanks.

CONTENTS

1

THE VENEERING ART

Veneering is an ancient art. Veneered items have been taken from the tombs of the Egyptian Pharoahs and some examples of plywood furniture have been discovered dating back to 1500 years before Christ. In the early civilizations many different materials—ivory, pearl shell, tortoise shell, precious metals, and precious stones—were used as veneers to cover surfaces of baser mediums. Veneering required enormous skill and years of training and was considered one of the fine arts. Until the early 1700's only the wealthy could afford pieces of veneered furniture. However, improved navigation made available fine woods from inaccessible locations, machines were developed that could perform some of the most difficult operations in the production of veneers, and veneered furniture became increasingly popular.

Many of the old cabinet makers used veneers to embellish their work. In the Carolean period (1660-1668) oak was largely used for the base wood with walnut, then considered a semi-precious wood, used as veneer.

The William and Mary era (1688-1702) saw the use of much marquetry—a form of veneering in which various colors and shapes of veneers were inlaid to form pictures, generally of a floral nature.

In the Queen Anne (1702-1714) and Georgian (1714-1760) periods veneering was much employed on the splats of fiddleback chairs and on the flats of chests. In the Louis XV period (1715-

1

1774) many different species of woods came into use as veneer. Notable among them were box, holly, kingwood, sycamore, and laburnum.

Chippendale (1705-1779) used veneers on the panels of doors, especially in his "French" period. Veneer was commonly used in Adam furniture, and was often emphasized by painting the surrounding areas.

Hepplewhite (?-1786) used Amboyna burls as veneer almost to the exclusion of any other species, with the exception of an occasional use of fine mahogany. Veneering was extensively employed during the Empire period (1793-1830); in America, almost invariably pine was used as the base wood, but in Europe, mahogany was veneered with the finest stump mahogany, meticulously matched, and many excellent pieces still exist in perfect condition.

In the middle 1800's the "Grand Rapids" type of furniture came into production in an attempt to meet the tremendous demand for house furnishings. In the factories of that time, mass production was the watchword and handwork was at a minimum. Cheap and cheaper materials were used, and poor and poorer craftsmanship was employed. Something had to be done to cover the shoddy workmanship and the poor materials, so veneers were glued over the panels to hide what was underneath. It was due to this unfortunate practice that fine furniture lost its reputation and the art of veneering fell into disrepute. Except to the informed, veneered furniture is still considered to be not as valuable or as durable as furniture made from "honest lumber." Actually, veneered furniture is much more durable. Given normal care, veneered articles will pass on down through the years without warping, splitting, coming apart at the seams, or showing cracks, shakes, or checks. It is only within the last few decades that plywood—for veneered panels, being made up of at least three layers or plys of wood, are in the true sense plywood—has come into its own.

Plywood falls into two main categories: construction panels and furniture plywood. Construction panels, generally made of fir, are used in wall sheathing, roofs, underlayment of floors, prefabricated houses—anywhere a strong, light, easily applied panel is desired. Today, in fact, entire homes are made of different kinds of plywood. Construction is fast and the finished house is strong—stronger, even, than an identical house made of solid lumber—and considerably cheaper in cost.

Panels come in different types for different uses: for interior use, with waterproof glue for exterior application, good one side, good both sides, and in a great number of thicknesses, from $\frac{1}{8}$ inch to several inches thick. The standard panel is 4 feet by 8 feet in size, but any number of different sizes are available, either as stock items or to order.

Furniture plywood panels are those which have the face and sometimes the back veneered in rare and exotic woods. They are used not only in furniture manufacture but also for wall panelling in homes, in offices, and in public buildings. It is this type of panel with which this volume specifically deals; commercial plywood is used here only as a core stock in order to produce the more ornamental material. However, few people know that plywood is superior for many uses, and even fewer are aware of the many operations that go into the manufacture of plywood panels. Since, in effect, the making of veneered furniture is the making of plywood, the veneersman should have at least a superficial knowledge of the construction and uses of commercial plywood.

The manufacture of the veneer itself is as fascinating as any adventure story. No forest or jungle in the world is so forbidding that men have not penetrated its fastness in search of exotic trees for the veneer industry. Rare trees do not grow in vast tracts as do the pines, fir, spruce, and other commoner woods. Here and there a solitary giant will rear its height in obscurity, until the hardwood seeker discovers it and it is felled to be shipped to a veneer mill.

Felling the tree, however, is the least of the battle. Getting the logs out of the jungle is the real task. Every method of transporta-

Chain-sawing hickory for veneers in our Southern forests.
U.S. Forestry Service. Courtesy Fine Hardwoods Association.

tion is used. In Burma elephants haul the teak logs out to the waterways. Logs are snaked to rivers by ox team or by tractor, where available—or by human labor where nothing else can approach. Then the logs are floated down to the seacoast where they can be loaded on steamers to bring them to the United States or other countries for processing.

After arrival at the mills, the logs are stored until needed for slicing into veneers. Generally the huge trees are stored in water, confined in large "tanks"—areas in the river or harbor with piling fences arranged to keep the logs from floating away. Storing under water keeps the logs from splitting and drying out unevenly, which would cause shakes and checks to appear through the timber.

When ready to be cut into veneer, a log is pulled from the storage tanks and started through the process of manufacture. Veneers are cut in several different ways, the most common being plain slicing.

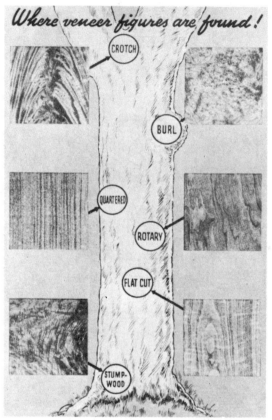

Note that crotch veneers are always shown and used in an inverted position from that in which they are found in the tree.

The logs are soaked in very hot water for several hours, or several days, depending on the hardness of the wood. They may be boiled for a time or immersed in steam baths. This heating softens the wood enough to enable it to be sliced in the cutters. After steaming, the logs are fastened into the slicing machine and a huge knife, up to 17 feet in length, is rigidly held in position while the log, securely fastened onto the carrier, is brought down against the cutting edge. After each stroke the carriage holding the log is

DIFFERENT WAYS IN WHICH VENEERS ARE CUT

The manner in which veneers are cut is an important factor in producing the various visual effects obtained. Two logs of the same species, but with their veneers cut differently, will have entirely different visual characters even though their colors are similar.

In veneer manufacture, five principle methods of cutting veneers are used.

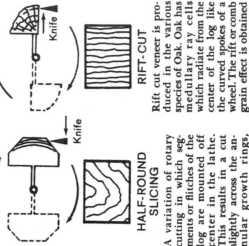

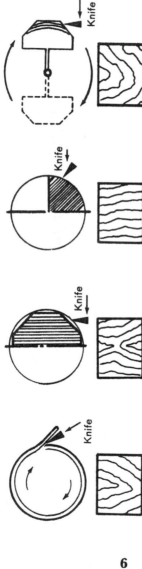

ROTARY

The log is mounted centrally in the lathe and turned against a razor sharp blade, like unwinding a roll of paper. Since this cut' follows the log's annular growth rings, a bold variegated grain marking is produced. Rotary cut veneer is exceptionally wide.

FLAT SLICING

The half log, or flitch, is mounted with the heart side flat against the guide plate of the slicer and the slicing is done parallel to a line through the center of the log. This produces a variegated figure.

QUARTER SLICING

The quarter log or flitch is mounted on the guide plate so that the growth rings of the log strike the knife at approximately right angles, producing a series of stripes, straight in some woods, varied in others.

HALF-ROUND SLICING

A variation of rotary cutting in which segments or flitches of the log are mounted off center in the lathe. This results in a cut slightly across the annular growth rings, and visually shows modified characteristics of both rotary and plain sliced veneers.

RIFT-CUT

Rift cut veneer is produced in the various species of Oak. Oak has medullary ray cells which radiate from the center of the log like the curved spokes of a wheel. The rift or comb grain effect is obtained by cutting perpendicularly to these medullary rays either on the lathe or slicer.

Besides the methods shown, certain very hard woods are sawn instead of sliced. Usually sawn veneers are thicker than those from a slicing machine.

advanced the thickness of the veneer much in the fashion of a meat slicing machine. The usual thickness is $\frac{1}{28}$ inch, although veneers are also sliced as thin as $\frac{1}{100}$ inch, and thicker than $\frac{1}{28}$ inch.

When a log is so long as to make slicing impossible, it is sawn into sheets, generally about $\frac{1}{20}$ inch thick. Slicing is preferred to sawing, however, because of the great loss of wood resulting from the thickness of the saw kerf, the notch made by the saw. Generally veneer is sawn on a travelling-carriage machine, being fed into a special segmented circular saw blade, or sometimes into a very large bandsaw.

The second method of producing veneers is quarter-slicing. Here the log is first cut in half, then in quarters, each length being pie-shaped. The sheets are then sliced across the growth rings from the outside to the heart.

Rotary-cutting is extensively employed in making veneer for plywood, rather than fine veneers for facing panels. All of the common fir plywood used in construction is rotary-cut. In this method the log is chucked into huge lathes and a flat sheet stripped from it as the log is revolved against the knife, much like pulling wrapping paper from a roll. The endless sheet is cut and stacked as it is peeled off the log, then sent through driers and made into plywood panels. It is rarely sold as veneer. Crotches, stumps, burls, and other unusual growths are always sliced flat or half round, rather than quarter cut. And there are other methods of cutting veneers specially used to suit special conditions.

From the slicer, the sheets of veneer, (which have been carefully kept in the exact order in which they were sliced from flitch) are sent to the trimmer, and thence to a drying machine, where controlled drying removes the excess moisture. Still in order, the veneer is stacked into the complete flitches, and either crated or bound with metal bands and stored until needed. A sample sheet is taken from each flitch and placed on display in the company's showroom for purchasers to examine. Sometimes a collection of sample sheets is sent to prospective purchasers. The veneer is sold

Slicing veneer on a hydraulic skew knife cutter.

Bandsaw preparing log for veneer slicer.

Mounting log on lathe for half-round slicing.

Stacking veneer sheets as they fall from the knife of the half-round lathe.

Removing veneer from dryer.

A commercial veneer trimmer capable of handling work as long as 17 feet and more!

Crating veneer.
Courtesy Fine Hardwoods Association

Veneer storage.

9

from this examination of samples which have been numbered to correspond with the numbers assigned to the flitch when it is put in stock.

As a rule the largest purchasers of veneers are furniture manufacturers, piano manufacturers, and commercial plywood companies. It takes an alert individual craftsman to get a jump ahead of the large consumers in order to obtain choice veneers for himself. I have tried, more or less unsuccessfully, for a number of years, to get ahead of the Steinway Piano Company in order to obtain a stock of choice Macassar ebony. Almost automatically all the top quality ebony goes to Steinway, leaving only that material which is full of checks and cracks or otherwise undesirable for fine work.

Often a flitch is taken to a salesroom and opened on the floor. There smaller quantities are sold to individual craftsmen who could not use or could not afford to purchase the entire flitch. When this is the case, the veneer is generally sold consecutively from the top sheets down. This is to avoid mixing up the order in which the sheets came from the log. Only by keeping the original order can the patterns and grain be matched with accuracy.

Plywood is a term generally used to designate glued-wood panels made up of two or more layers of veneer, with the grain of adjacent layers at right angles to each other. Most plywood contains an odd number of layers, e.g., three, five, seven, or more. Occasionally a thin panel may be made of only two layers, but this is weak and of little use except as a backing device for very rare veneers backed with a strong material instead of another sheet of veneer. These 2-ply sheets are then treated as a single thickness and glued into regular plywood panels.

Wood shrinks or expands as its moisture content changes. This shrinkage is greater across the grain, almost nonexistent *along* the grain. Also, wood has considerably more strength in one direction than in the other. A good example of this is offered anyone who tries to drive a nail into a board too close to the end: the board usually splits along the grain. Plywood is often called "balanced

construction" because the tendency to split along the grain is balanced out in the manner in which a panel is made.

The foundation for all plywood is the core. This is the center
layer, or ply; it may be made of fairly thick lumber, or a sheet of
veneer. If veneer is used, the core ply is generally thicker than the
remaining layers. Common woods are mostly used for the cores,
and those which have a low coefficient of shrinkage are the most
desirable, because the finished panel is less likely to warp.

After the cores are prepared the crossbands and face and back
veneers are ready to be glued in place. If the panel under construction is to be 3-ply, the face and back veneers are glued directly to the core. If thicker panels are being manufactured, then
alternate layers of veneer are glued to the core in the second step
of manufacture. The grain of each layer must run at right angles
to the grain of the layer before it. That is, the core with its grain
running the long way of the panel is glued between two sheets of
veneer which have the grain running across the width. The next
two sheets applied have the grain running the same direction as
the core, and so on. When the panels are being built, attention
must be paid to the direction the face veneer wants to run, and the
direction of the core grain adjusted accordingly. If one were making 3-ply panels the core would run the short dimension to start.
In 5-ply panels the core would run the long dimension, the crossbanding or intermediate layers with short grain, and the face and
back veneers long again. One can readily see the advantages to this
type of construction. If wood wants to shrink and warp across the
grain, the layers running in the opposite direction prohibit this,
resulting in a "balanced" panel that has much greater dimensional
stability than solid lumber.

After the core is made and the face and back veneer sheets
prepared, the core is run through a machine having top and bottom rollers that feed glue in an even spread onto both sides at the
same time. As the glued core leaves the machine it is layed over a
back veneer, and topped with a face veneer. The back veneer has
been placed on a *caul*—a waxed or oiled board as large or larger

Construction of a commercial lumber-core panel, showing the direction of grain in the different layers. *Courtesy Fine Hardwoods Association*

than the panel and true and flat, or a sheet of metal. Glued panels are piled with a caul between each pair of panels and a last caul on top of the stack. The entire stack is then fed into a press that compresses the plywood to express excess glue, and to hold all firmly in place while the glue-line cures and sets. Modern presses are heated. The modern resin glues would take eight to ten hours to harden if merely put under pressure at ordinary temperatures; in a heated press they will cure in from two to six *minutes,* depending on the temperature of the platens!

Another kind of press is one in which the glue-line is cured by the action of high-frequency electrical waves. This again is a high-speed operation, and one that is coming more and more into commercial use.

A third method of gluing panels is with thin dry sheets of resin film. These films are placed between the layers of veneer, and when the panel is put into the heated press, the film is melted and forced into the pores of the veneer to make a tight bond. Most of the fine furniture today is made by this method. Chairs are about the only exception, and even the back splats and seats of many chairs are of laminated panels.

Besides the inherent stability of veneered panels, the cabinet-maker today has available woods of breath-taking beauty which cannot be found in solid lumber. Burls, crotches, stumps, stripes, whorls,—an almost unlimited procession of fancy figures and grains are at his command in the form of thin sheets of veneer. By careful and judicious matching, the complicated figures in veneer can be made even more elaborate. Book-matching, quarter-matching, slip-and-butt-matching, and combinations of these make possible a truly formidable array of patterns, textures, and colors.

With the development of modern methods, up-to-date gluing techniques, and resin glues, nothing stands in the way of the cabinetmaker producing articles of furniture that a century ago could only have been possessed by a king, emperor, or very wealthy individual.

Veneering requires the use of a few special tools that are peculiar to this work alone. Burls especially are often full of holes and other defects, because of the manner of growth, and patching and repairing before use is not only desirable but mandatory. Special punches having irregular shapes are available for the patching of veneer. They have a spring-loaded ejector to push out the punched wafer, and are used on a block of end-grain hardwood.

These punches are made in Europe and are rather difficult to find in the United States, though the H. L. Wild Company in New York City carries them and maintains a mail order service for hard-to-find tools for veneering. The reason for the odd shapes of veneering punches is that an irregular line is difficult to see, and when the joint is well made the patch is virtually invisible; whereas a patch with a regular outline, such as square or round, would stand out vividly as soon as the finish was applied.

Many burls are unobtainable without holes and defects, and the fact that a piece of furniture made from such burls may be patched is in no way detrimental to the quality or appearance of the article. Indeed persons owning a well-made article of furniture are likely to find a patch or two if the veneer used is a burl. And he may have had the article for years without noticing the patch, the outline of which was blended so skillfully into the overall pattern of the grain.

2

GLUES AND ADHESIVES

There are many different kinds of adhesives that can be used for veneering. In the days before modern resin adhesives, hide glue was about the only material available to the veneer worker. This was cumbersome to use, the room had to be kept very warm, the glue was worked hot, and the veneer and core had to be heated just before spreading the glue. Then the rush to get the panel into the press and the press tightened up before the glue-line cooled was taxing and exhausting work. The messy labor and the unhandiness of heating everything was likely responsible to a large degree for the unpopularity of veneering in small shops or by the home craftsman.

Today, however, all this has been changed radically with the advent of chemical bonding materials. In the beginning of the development of these new and useful adhesives, casein glues were used extensively. Indeed, they were the forerunners of the present assortment of adhesives now marketed.

Cascin glues had the troublesome faculty of staining certain woods, especially mahogany and oak, sometimes to the point where the work could be ruined if the worker was unable to exercise special precautions against getting glue on the surface or having it seep out the glue-line after the panel was in the press. The only way some work could be reclaimed was to stain it a color darker than the glue-line, but since most of the beauty of veneered work is in the natural color and figure of the veneer, staining is most undesirable.

Casein glue came as a powder to be mixed with water just before using. It had many advantages over hot hide glue in that there was no necessity to heat the cauls, core, or veneer, and the worker did not have to work in a sweat-box to keep the glue from setting before the pressure was applied. It had a much longer pre-use life than hot glue, and after mixing was usable for several hours before setting became a problem. The use of casein glue allowed the veneersman to take up to 15 or 20 minutes to get the work spread, assembled, and in the press, a time that was greatly in excess of that allowable with hot hide glue.

Casein glue has been generally superseded by urea resin glues. Urea resins are most handy to use. They do not stain, their colors for the most part are much lighter than the color of casein glues, and for that reason are more useful in veneering light woods such as avodire, limba, and satinwood.

Many companies make urea resins, which come in two forms. Large commercial plants use urea resin as a double-unit product: that is, the adhesive is a thick viscous liquid, which, before use, is mixed with a powder catalyst and hardener. Sometimes fillers are added to extend the glue. This kind of adhesive is generally used in very large quantities and mixed in heavy machines. The process is almost entirely automated: the glue is mixed and fed to the spreading machine, which applies it to one or both surfaces of the work simultaneously; the panels are then fed into heated presses where the glue is cured in a matter of minutes.

For our purpose we are concerned with the second type of urea resin, that which is supplied as a powder with the catalyst, and with or without extenders, already combined. This powder is mixed with water shortly before application and has a working life of a few hours before setting progresses too far.

Powdered urea resins are obtainable in small amounts, from $\frac{1}{4}$-pound cans to 25-pound cans and larger. Thus it is easy to buy just the quantity that is best for your size operation. Since the glue keeps for only about a year, it is better to purchase smaller containers and replace with fresh stock as you run out. I have settled on the 25-pound cans as a compromise between economy—it is cheaper as the size increases—and the shelf-life of the powder.

There are several brands available, but Cascamite and Weldwood are the best known. I use Weldwood because I find it a bit easier to mix and use, but possibly this is just a personal preference.

The principal uses of urea resin adhesives are for interior materials where the work is not to be subjected to the action of the weather. The glue-line is water resistant; normal or even somewhat excessive humidity will not affect it, but as an exterior adhesive it is not practical. It is excellent for gluing any porous material, but does not hold to metals. It is unaffected by oil, gasoline, or solvents after setting, and insects and fungi do not readily attack it. A good quality is that lacquer does not affect the glue-line, as is the case with some of the modern adhesives. These tend to swell at the glue-line as lacquer is applied, which causes the finish to craze and makes necessary a second sanding and application of lacquer.

The working life of Weldwood is ample for all veneer work in the small shop. At 70 degrees F. the mixed glue will keep for from 4 to 5 hours and during use the craftsman has from 15 to 25 minutes to get the work coated and in the press. This time lessens as the temperature increases; at 90 degrees the pot-life of the glue is only 1 to 2 hours, and the assembly time 5 to 8 minutes.

The time required under pressure is also affected by temperature. Thus, at 70 degrees the press time is 12 hours, and at 90 degrees, it is cut to 5 hours for complete curing. The glue-line does not reach maximum curing, however, for several days after pressing. The panels may be worked the day after having been removed from the press and stacked on end with clear air circulation around them over night to allow the moisture content in the glue to distribute and equalize.

The optimum mixture for Weldwood is 10 parts powder to 6 parts water by *weight*. I keep an old scale in the glue room and a large stainless steel bowl obtained from the supermarket. The scale is set to read zero with the empty bowl on the platen. This is the "tare" adjustment. The powdered glue is now poured into the bowl until the proper weight is reached. Remember that the proportion of 10 glue to 6 water is to be maintained regardless of the total amount you are mixing. Pour in the water, watching the scale dial until about half of the required weight of water has been added. Mix the glue and water thoroughly into a stiff paste. Then return the bowl to the scale and add the remainder of the water to make up the total weight. Mix again until the glue is a smooth and creamy liquid. I find that if you add about one half the water and mix the glue thoroughly into a thick paste, then add the second half of the water and continue mixing, you arrive at a smoother mixture less liable lump up. In any event, it is good practice to let the glue stand for a half-hour or so after mixing, then mix again until all the small lumps that have collected on the surface are broken down into liquid.

Both the glue and the water should be measured by weight rather than by volume.

Polyvinyl resin glues are available as liquids that have a few uses in the veneer shop. They are not good for gluing up panels, but are excellent for repairing or for gluing small pieces in place after veneering has been completed. Polyvinyl resins are also useful for inlaying border strips and marquetry. These glues are white milky fluids which turn clear and transparent upon drying. They set very quickly and do not allow the worker much time to assemble the work before becoming tacky.

Resorcin resins are the well known "marine" glues, or water-proof adhesives. They are dark red in color and stain badly. They have not much application in the veneer shop, but are useful in boat building or in assembling panels of veneered stock which are to be subjected to dampness. Extreme care must be taken not to get resorcin resin glue on the surface of the work. Nor should it be used on light-colored veneers with an open grain, where there is possibility of forcing the glue through the pores. Stains caused by resorcin resins cannot be removed from pale veneers. It is also difficult to remove from the metal press blankets.

A useful adhesive for veneer work is Urac 185. This is a liquid urea formaldehyde resin which is mixed with a powder catalyst and hardening agent before use. It is manufactured by American Cyanamid Company and has a number of very useful and distinctive properties.

Urac 185 has a low shrinkage coefficient, which makes it useful for gluing surfaces that cannot be tightly fitted, since the glue fills the interstices and inequalities. This is not to say that you can turn out poorly fitted work and depend on the adhesive to fill in the bad spots. What it does mean, however, is that in places where good clamping is difficult or impossible, you *can* make a good bond and a tight joint with the use of this adhesive. Since the shrinkage is so low, it does not craze as much as other glues, which in turn makes possible a thicker glue-line than normally obtainable. If the work cannot be brought up into extreme tightness with clamps, Urac 185 will still make an excellent bond, with a somewhat thicker glue-line.

The shelf-life of Urac 185 it about the same as that of Weld-wood and other urea resins. It should be mixed just before use, and a little more care exercised in loading the press, because the glue is more difficult to remove from the metal plates. All spills should be removed from the plates and care taken not to scratch the plates in the process.

Where Urac 185 comes into its own in the small shop is in gluing curved and irregularly shaped work. With work that is difficult to clamp tightly without a very complicated setup and special clamp design, Urac 185 will give a secure and tight joint under conditions that are something less than optimum.

Urac 185 is also very useful in veneering oily woods such as ebony, paldao, teak, and yew, with a minimum of surface treatment when applied. Generally these woods are difficult to glue because of the great amount of oil in them. Some, teak for example, will often snap right off the panel after gluing because the glue did not penetrate the oil sufficiently to make a good bond. In these extreme cases the craftsman has recourse to several expedients. The easiest is to score the gluing surface heavily with a sharp knife or very rough sandpaper just before applying the glue. With Urac 185 this may be enough to supply a tooth for the glue bond. In scoring veneer, remember that you have about one half the thickness of the veneer to work with. When the cuts are too deep they may possibly show on the surface after sanding the finished work. Slanting cuts to actually raise little kerfs is the best way of scoring. This allows the glue to get under the layers and make a good bond.

I have found that a sponge wet with lacquer-thinner is useful in removing the oil from the surface of teak and other very oily woods. After I have everything set up for gluing, I wash the inside surface of the back veneer with the lacquer-thinner, then apply the glue to the core and put it in place. I then wash the gluing surface of the face veneer, apply the second coat of glue and slide everything into the press, clamping up as fast as possible to keep the oil from returning to the surface.

Another expedient that can be used in extreme cases where the oil is very bad—some flitches of teak and paldao are saturated—is to wash as before with the lacquer-thinner, then lay a layer of thin muslin or cheesecloth on the glue surface before assembly. You must be sure that the material is stretched out evenly and smoothly to avoid pressing folds under the veneer which would be certain to telegraph through to the surface. The addition of a cloth layer can only be done when the edges of the work are to be hidden, either by being veneered or by becoming part of a hidden joint.

Before gluing up some rare burls of thuya, I have on several occasions been forced to resort to actually soaking the veneers in lacquer-thinner for a couple of hours, then in alcohol for another few hours, finally drying them between many thicknesses of newspaper. I had great good fortune to find one of these burls with a figure to defy all imagination. However, it was so oily that a depression made with a finger nail would actually make a wet spot. Only by soaking in lacquer-thinner and alcohol was I able to use the veneer. The panels have been glued up for several years now, and are as flat and tight as when they came out of the press. Picking at the edges does not loosen them, and the glue-line—I used Urac 185 for this—has shown no deterioration to date.

Fish glues and liquid hide glues such as LePage's and other brands do not find much use in the veneering shop. They are more for household and hobby use, and while they might be excellent adhesives, their cost and application make them impractical for large veneering operations. They are of value, however, in small patch-repairs; if a flake of veneer has been snapped off an edge or corner, it is more practical to fix it in place with a prepared glue rather than to mix a small quantity of the regular adhesive.

In recent years an adhesive has been developed for applying plastic laminates to plywood panels. This is a contact adhesive and makes a very strong and permanent bond when correctly applied. This rubber-based adhesive is applied to both surfaces, preferably two coats to each, then allowed to dry until it is no longer tacky.

21

The two surfaces are then brought into contact and they adhere to each other as soon as they touch.

Great care must be taken to position the work accurately, because on contact they are bonded together—for good! The worker does not get two chances to align his work.

After putting the work together, the entire surface must be subjected to some sort of pressure to afford a complete contact bond. In most instances, pounding the surface with a rubber mallet is quite sufficient. A roller can be used if the craftsman can obtain enough pressure with it. Or the work, if flat, may be slid into the press with the screws run up tight for one or two minutes, then removed from the press immediately. After the initial contact and pressure there is no further curing necessary to make the permanent bond.

For veneering the edges of panels this type of adhesive is excellent. It eliminates the need for very long bar clamps and the use of pressure bars to hold the veneer in place. The disadvantage of contact adhesive for edge work is the fact that the glue is softened by lacquer and lacquer-thinner, and unless great care is taken to sand every speck of adhesive from the glue-line before finishing, there is apt to be a swelling and seepage of glue after the lacquer is applied. This may be sanded off and the work relacquered, but it means an extra operation and more time. If care is taken to use thin coats of adhesive, evenly applied, and the work given a good pounding with the mallet or very tight clamping, the chance of glue seepage is minimal; the great ease with which the veneer can be applied to the edges, especially curved and angular edges, more than outweighs the extra labor involved.

Another most valuable application of contact adhesives is in the reveneering of a surface of an already assembled article of furniture. Once in a while a chest or other piece of furniture which has been completed and in service for a while suffers such damage to a face that it would be ruined if repair was not possible. It would be out of the question to disassemble the piece to reveneer the damaged panel; a piece of veneer glued to the surface of the assembled piece would probably cause that surface to warp out of control due to the pulling and expansion of only one surface of the panel. With the use of contact adhesive, however, the item may often be saved. This does not put any warp into the panel, because there is no water in the adhesive to penetrate the wood and cause swelling and/or shrinkage. Since the veneer itself is not under the strain of water absorption, it remains dormant and does not attempt to move as the glue sets. The work does not have to be put through the veneer press, so the repair can be made on the standing cabinet with light but thorough pounding with a rubber mallet to make the bond. The additional thickness of the repair layer of veneer will most often go unnoticed in the completed work, and the entire work can be refinished to blend the colors of the old and the new veneers. Of course, this type of repair can only be done if you have some of the original veneer left in stock, or if you are lucky enough to find some veneer that very nearly if not exactly matches that which was used in the beginning.

3

CLAMPS AND CLAMPING

Surprisingly enough, the craftsman most often runs into difficulty in the clamping of assemblies, or in assembling curved work, rather than in the manipulation of the veneers, or in the laying-up of the panels. Much of this difficulty occurs because he does not make a "dry run" before putting the work in glue. Often he will carry his work right up to the time to spread the glue and start the assembly, and then discover to his dismay that the clamps at hand will not fit, will not hold on an irregular surface, or cannot accommodate the shape of the piece he is working on. Then the scramble begins to try to get some kind of pressure on the glue-lines before everything sets up. Disaster is often the result. Dry runs and a complete trial assembly, even putting the clamps in place and tightening them, will eliminate this kind of hazard and make the final assembly-in-glue that much easier, especially if you are working alone.

It is excellent practice when cutting curved work, the edges of which are to be veneered, to number or otherwise index the offfall and the work, keeping the two together so you can use the waste piece as a clamping caul when the edge veneer is glued in place. It is very difficult to cut an irregularly shaped clamping bar to exactly fit the shape of the work, but the waste piece can generally be easily matched to the working edge. Also, it affords a flat side against which the clamps can be brought to bear to eliminate slippage when tightening them up.

A very important thing to remember when clamping irregular work is that the clamping pressure must be at right angles to the glue-line, or the work will slip. The best way to be sure that your clamps are pulling true is to cut steps in the outer surface of the clamping cauls with the "tread" of the steps parallel to the glue-line directly under the pressure point. If it is impossible to cut steps on the other side of the piece you are assembling, then wedges can be placed under the ends of the clamps. To keep the wedges from slipping out from under the clamps, tack them in place with a small brad or glue them directly to the surface of the work, with a paper between the wedges and the work. After the work has been clamped and the glue set, the wedges can easily be sawn off close to the surface, and the remaining layer sanded off with no damage to the work itself. This method of gluing clamping steps to the work is an old one and is used extensively in gluing up mitered corners in furniture-making. The importance of having the clamp pressure parallel to the glue-line cannot be overstressed. The slightest angle out of line may cause the veneer to slip on the glue layer when the pressure is applied, and since the work is concealed by the caul or clamping bar, it is too late to do anything about it when the glue has set and the clamps are removed. Taping the veneer is no insurance, because under the enormous pressure of the clamps the tape can easily tear and allow the veneer to slip.

There are clamps for almost every conceivable application. One difficult operation is edge-veneering. The narrow strips are hard to hold in place, and the work is generally too long to allow one person to easily span both ends at the same time in order to hold the clamping bars in place. The veneer tends to slip off the edges because it is most difficult to be certain that both clamping bars and all the clamps are exactly parallel to the edge surfaces. If you have two or more assistants who can hold all the veneer strips and clamping bars in place while you run up the clamps, the work is a bit easier. But this is not always possible. One way around this problem is to use short strips of masking tape to hold the veneer in place. Then position the clamping bars across horses, lay the panel in between the bars, and gently take up the slack on the clamps just enough to hold all in place while you check position and angles before tightening everything up. Strips of thin wood are placed across the horses under the panel, but not under the clamping bars, to raise up the panel being clamped to center on the clamping bars. Additional strips are placed on the top of the panel to hold the bar clamps from the surface when pulling them up tight. If the bar of the clamp rested on the face of the panel, the clamp jaws would be off center and be liable to pull the clamping bar to one side or the other when the pressure was applied.

You must be careful to save all the trimmings when cutting out an irregularly shaped panel that is going to be edge-veneered. These trimmings should be indexed so they can be used in exactly the same space they came from. As a general rule, if the cutting of the shape was accurate enough, the saw kerf will be just right to allow for the thickness of the edge veneer, and the off-fall or trimming can merely be pushed into place over the veneer to act as a clamping caul. If it is possible to cut the outer edges of the trimmings into a circle or ellipse, then a *band clamp* may be used to advantage. These are manufactured in several different widths and almost any length desired. Two types are available—one with heavy fabric bands, and the other with thin steel bands. The steel bands are intended mainly for production factories, where the work is uniformly shaped and hundreds or thousands of a kind are manufactured. The fabric bands are easier for the small craftsman to use because of the greater flexibility of the heavy canvas and they are more easily stored, rolled up into a small coil.

Band clamps will pull up very tight, and find use in such operations as edging round tables, oval tables, or even the ends of long rectangular work with the help of pressure cauls between the band and the work. Such cauls must have the ends rounded to allow the band to slip as it tightens, and not cut on the sharp corner. It stands to reason that band clamps can not be used on square or rectangular work, since the bands would either cut themselves on

Always place bar clamps on opposite sides of a panel to keep from bowing
the work. *Courtesy Adjustable Clamp Company*

the corners, pull up the veneers, or slack off at the sharp bends.
Steel band clamps are intended for clamping round or oval shapes
only.

Many different styles and sizes of bar clamps are available for
edge-clamping. *Piling clamps* are a clever type of double action
bar clamp that pull up panels of core stock in stacks, clamping the
top and the bottom of adjacent panels at the same time. They are
very handy to use if you make your own core panels out of lumber.

If a number of panels the same width are to be made up at the
same time, a simple stacking clamp—to hold up to six or eight
panels simultaneously—may be made out of two lengths of ¾- or 1-
inch pipe and a supply of hardwood boards about 18 inches longer
than the width of the panels. Bore a hole just large enough to
receive the pipe about 4 inches in from each end of each board. As
these holes should be the same distance apart on all the boards, use
one for a jig to bore all the others from. Nail a short cleat across
the ends of the boards just touching the *outside* edges of the holes.
This is to back up the pipe when pressure is applied. Next
cut a supply of wedges, allowing two wedges for each board. To
use the clamp is very easy. Lay a pair of the boards on a level part

of the floor and stand the two pipe lengths upright in the holes. The pipes should be about 3 feet long at most.

When all the core strips for the panels have been prepared, glue up the first set and lay them across the boards. Put a scrap strip of wood about an inch wide on one side of the panel and slide the whole affair tightly against one of the pipes. Slide a second board over the pipes and down on top of the panel assembly. Then, using the wedges in pairs so as not to mar the edges of the cores, drive them in tightly between the edge of the panel assembly and the second pipe. The two boards will hold the pipe firmly against the pressure, and you can drive the components of the panel together as tight as you can pull them with bar clamps.

The second core may now be laid on top of the second clamp board, a scrap strip put in place as before, another clamp board slid down over the pipes and, again, a pair of wedges driven home. You may continue in this fashion until the stacking clamp is filled with core panels. If you make the clamping boards long enough, they may also be used to glue up a number of different widths of panels simply by using filler strips on the sides for the narrower panels. Made out of oak, maple, or birch, the clamping boards will last for years.

Handscrews are used when clamping up inlay border strips, or border veneers. They, in conjunction with distribution cauls, are applied all around the edges of a panel, and an entire inlay border may be glued at the same time by positioning the cauls so they do not interfere with each other. Handscrews supply considerable pressure when properly adjusted, but can and do cause slippage if fastened to the work out of parallel. It should become a habit to adjust the clamp by tightening the outer screw only, exercising care to see that the jaws are exactly parallel before applying the final pressure.

Handscrews come in many sizes. The most useful ones for veneer work are the small 00 and 000, and the medium #2. Even the small sizes can apply astonishing amounts of pressure. The 000 clamps are particularly useful in gluing inlay strips around the edges of panels. They open just enough to take a panel and a clamping caul, and are easy to handle when you have a panel bristling with a dozen or more clamps stuck around the sides. When opening or closing handscrews to adjust them to the work, you should always start by first making sure that the jaws are parallel. Then, taking a handle in each hand, roll your hands exactly the same way you would move your feet when pedalling a bicycle; the clamp will open rapidly, and the jaws will remain parallel. Adjust the clamp to barely clear the work it is to be put on, and then bring it into snug position by turning the inner screw. The final pressure can be applied by operating the outer screw, and the jaws should be checked as you go to make sure you are keeping them parallel. It cannot be stressed too often that it is absolutely necessary to adjust clamps so that the pressure points are at right angles to the glue-line, and that the jaws of handscrews are parallel before tightening them.

A *miter clamp* is a small bar clamp with a pair of bosses on the clamping jaws. These bosses are intended to be inserted in holes bored in the underside of the work to be clamped, and will pull up a mitered corner easily and accurately without the necessity of using long bar clamps and/or a clamping jig. However, miter clamps are intended for use on joints where the undersides will not be seen in the finished piece and the piece is made of solid lumber. (A hole drilled in the edge of plywood will easily pull out when the clamp is tightened.) Miter clamps do not have too much value in veneering, although they are of some use in making furniture, especially where frames, drawer frames, and similar work is to be clamped on a miter joint.

Long-reach bar clamps are most useful when you are inlaying in the centers of panels. If the panel is of a size that prohibits the use of a clamp, either a long-reach bar or a regular handscrew, the inlay may be clamped by the use of a slightly curved pressure caul faced with felt or heavy cardboard. This is merely a piece of wood wide enough to cover the entire inlay, planed slightly convex along the clamping edge, then faced with a material that will take up any inequalities in the work, different thicknesses in the inlay, or variation on the edge of the caul itself. A most useful material for clamping bars and cauls is a sheet of ¼ inch thick *Homasote,* or underlayment board. This is in reality just very heavy, firm cardboard, and strips may be sawn to fit your bars and glued to them permanently. With a convex pressure caul to reach across the panel and a straight caul of the same dimensions on the reverse side, to keep the panel from being bent to fit the pressure caul instead of the caul bending to apply center pressure, you may clamp up a center inlay with two large handscrews at the ends of the cauls. Or you may use two long-reach bar clamps; or place the assembly inside of one frame of the veneer press and use two press screws without the pressure bars of the press, or the blankets. For inlays too far from the edge of a panel to use handscrews, I prefer, whenever possible, to use the veneer press, because of the greater pressure available. It is far easier to set a panel under a press frame than it is to position long-reach bar clamps. Use of a press frame is preferable also because of the ever-present possibility of springing the bar clamp, which would ruin the clamp for the work it was designed to do. However, a pair of these clamps should be kept in the shop for emergency use when it is impossible or undesirable for any reason to use the veneer press for clamping.

Large *C-clamps* are very useful for smaller work. In Europe these are called G-clamps, which name seems a bit more accurate, since the outline of the clamp resembles a G more than a C. They are made with a number of different throat depths, in a number of different sizes, in light-duty and heavy-duty types. For veneer work it pays to get only the heavy-duty kind, since the lighter ones may be sprung out of alignment under persistent hard use. Often C-clamps can be substituted for handscrews in gluing up inlay border strips, if the border is close enough to the edge of the panel to fall within the jaw reach of the clamps. They may also be alternated with handscrews if your supply of these is limited and insufficient to go around the work. Many times it is convenient to use a C-clamp to hold the caul in place while you adjust the handscrews.

If the C-clamp is put in place vertically, it has much less chance of causing slippage then the handscrew, and will serve admirably to hold the work until all the pressure has been applied. Then it can either be left in place as an added clamp, or removed, or moved to another position. While affording far less pressure than handscrews, still, if placed at close enough intervals, C-clamps will be fine for inlay strips, edge borders, and similar small-area veneering purposes.

Many times the necessity for clamping across a panel is combined with the need for downward pressure at the same time. For this purpose a *Cross-clamp fixture* is available. This is similar to a press screw, except that it slips over the bar of most bar clamps and tightens at right angles to the bar. Except when gluing up core stock out of lumber strips, where a slight bend in the individual strips must be pulled out in clamping up the core, cross-clamp fixtures have little use to the veneersman. When needed, however, they easily do a job that almost no other clamp will do, and can correct a situation which might otherwise make the job impossi-

Cross clamps will take any bow out of a clamped-up panel and are used to make all surfaces even while the glue cures.

Courtesy Adjustable Clamp Company

ble. They are ideal for clamping directly on the glue-line of core strips to make certain each pair of strips is level before clamping the core panel with the bar clamps.

Fast action clamps are merely a refinement of standard clamps and are intended to be run up to position without having to work the screw, which is turned after running-up only to tighten the clamp. They are fine if you are concerned with high-speed production, but not necessary for ordinary shop use.

Swivel clamps, which are fastened permanently in place along the bench that supports the work while it is under pressure, are useful if the craftsman is making many pieces the same size and shape. In this case the swivel clamps become a part of a gluing fixture and are part of a production tool for continued manufacture of similar items.

There are many, many more types of clamps: toggle clamps can be made into permanent fixtures for production work; hydraulic clamps for large areas and large shops; compound clamps, cam clamps. Literally hundreds of styles have been designed to meet special needs. They are, however, too numerous to be discussed here, and are of no special value to a veneering craftsman.

4

HOW TO BUILD YOUR
OWN VENEER PRESS

The most important tool used in veneering is the veneer press. In this machine you glue up your flat panels, and, by using certain types of cradles, you can even do various kinds of curved work. Commercial presses are fabulously expensive. Even a small one costs several thousand dollars, and a press large enough to do a 4 foot by 8 foot panel would run well over ten thousand dollars! Besides their cost, they are so huge that you would have to have a room about equal to a two-car garage to house the thing. Hydraulically operated and generally having heated platens, the commercial press is out of the question for the home craftsman.

However, with press screws and channel iron frames, one can put together a press well within the financial limits of the average craftsman, which will turn out professional panels for a lifetime. I have built two such presses at an individual cost of about three hundred and fifty dollars, which is a long way from ten thousand!

To fill the need of a practical method of gluing veneered panels, the Adjustable Clamp Company of Chicago, Illinois, manufactures a press screw designed especially for the assembly of veneer presses for school use, small shops, and the home craftsman. It is made in three sizes, but the 9-inch size is best for average use. The manufacturer recommends 1 screw to each 81 square inches of press area—in other words, 9 inches apart each way. This spacing may be adjusted somewhat to suit your convenience, but in no case should the press frames be spaced farther than 1 foot apart, nor the screws farther than 10 inches apart in the frames.

The press can be made almost any size you like. Bear in mind, however, that you must close the press fast, after the panel has been put in glue, and to do so you must reach across the press to tighten all the screws. If you make the press too wide and cumbersome, you will have difficulty in manipulating it. Also, remember that almost any piece of furniture, although it may be a large and massive piece, is made up of many small panels; the press you design might be quite considerably smaller than you at first think you will need, and still turn out all the work you want to do.

Unless you intend to make a large number of wide dining-room tables, for instance, or similar panels of large area, a press 2 feet wide and 9 feet long is ideal. Almost every cabinet you make will fall within these dimensions, and 90 per cent of them will be smaller by a good deal. With a press 9 feet long it would be possible to glue up the carcass of a very large cabinet in two loadings, the top and one end in one load, and the bottom and the other end in the second load. With smaller cabinets all four sections could be run up simultaneously. The widest panel used for most furniture is 20 inches, so you will have plenty space to spare around the edges.

The home veneer press is made up of any number of frames, lined up on a sturdy base and tied together with two or more stringers across the tops of the frames. The bed is made of panels of ¾-inch fir plywood laid on rails of 4 inch I-beams or 2 x 4's on edge. The blankets are sheets of hard-rolled aluminum, although in a pinch, a hard-surfaced wooden panel such as birch or maple plywood might be used with a sheet of kraft paper between the blanket and the work on both the top and the bottom.

Plywood blankets are so clumsy to use, and the paper is so apt to wrinkle under the loading that it is well worth the added expense to use the aluminum sheets. If the paper does pull up when you load the press, you will glue the panel fast between and to the blankets, and will end up with a solid block you can do nothing with.

The frames for a press are made up of four lengths of channel steel. For a press 2 feet by 9 feet, channel irons 1 inch by 2 inches with a $\frac{3}{16}$-inch web thickness is fine. This is a standard channel and is a stock item in almost every company that sells structural steel. They will cut it to length for a very nominal sum. The channels should be 6 inches longer than the inside width of the press, e.g., 30 inches long for the 2-foot press we are contemplating.

With the frames spaced 1 foot apart, you will need nine frames for a 9-foot press, because the first frame will be set in 6 inches from the end, as will the last. Each frame will require three press screws. To space the channels, and to supply a mount for the press screws, you will need eighteen lengths of hard maple, 2 inches wide, $1\frac{1}{2}$ inches thick, and the same length as the channels. These

A frame partly assembled, showing the component parts.

should be straight and true and free from knots or other weakening imperfections.

Nine assemblies are to be made up of a pair of channels bolted to a wood spacer. These are for the bottoms of the frames. Nine assemblies must also be made with the spacers bored to accept the press-screw nuts. For these assemblies, draw a line down the center of each spacer on the 1½-inch face. Measure in 1 inch from each end. Bore a ⅝-inch diameter hole through at these points for tie rods to assemble the frames. Half the spacers may be laid aside now, because no further treatment is necessary. The other half should be lined up accurately and marked in the center, then 9 inches each side of center. Bore three holes 1 inch in diameter through each spacer at these points. These are for the press-screw bushings, which must be pressed into place, but not until the spacer has been fastened between the channels.

When clamping a pair of channels to each spacer (the flat of the channel against the spacer), drill ¼-inch holes through both channels and the spacer about ½ inch each side of all the holes in the top assembly, and in the bottom assemblies. Bolt together tightly, using washers and lock washers under each nut.

If you have a method of pressing the screw nuts in place do so now. If you have no arbor press, then any machine shop will, for a moderate fee, press the bushings in place for you. They should be put in from the bottom of the assembly, and snugged down until the tabs on the bushings touch the metal of the channels.

Each frame will require two tie rods, 19 inches long and ⅝ inch in diameter. They must be threaded on both ends, which makes it practical to purchase lengths of threaded rod and cut them to length, rather than make up the rods out of round stock. Two spacers for each frame can be made of ordinary pipe. Each should be 13¼ inches long, and either black or galvanized ¾-inch pipe is fine. Eight ¾-inch washers and four ⅝-inch nuts complete the hardware for each frame.

To assemble a frame, thread a nut on the end of two tie rods until about ¼ inch of rod is through the nut. Drop a washer on top of each nut, then feed the tie rods through each end of a plain bottom assembly. Drop another washer on the rod, then a pipe spacer, topping that with a third washer. Then feed the top assembly in place, making certain that the bushings for the screws are on the bottom or inside of the assembly. The final washer is now put on, the remaining nuts threaded in place, and the whole assembly tightened up as much as possible. Assemble all the frames in this manner, then lay them aside while you make the base for your press.

The base is made out of 2 x 8 lumber, having outside dimensions of 2 feet by 9 feet 4 inches. Six legs should be bolted to the base, one on the inside of each corner, and two more on the inside

Make the base first and set it in the position it is to occupy before starting to assemble the press.

of the frame in the center of each side. Make these out of 4 x 4 lumber. Attach the legs with two ½-inch carriage bolts, and if the press is to be in a permanent position in your shop, putting glue on the legs before bolting them to the base would help to strengthen the whole affair.

To assemble the press, first place the base so you have space to walk all around it comfortably, making sure that it is level and steady. Position a frame on center, 8 inches in from one end, then

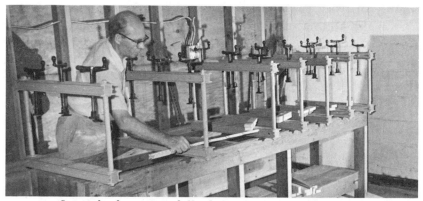

Space the frames carefully down the length of the base.

Cut the spacing cleats to fit snugly between the frames, then pivot them into position.

The spacing cleats can be screwed to the base to hold the frames firmly in position.

frames centered 1 foot apart all the way down the base. The last frame should end up 8 inches in from the back end of the press.

Cut wood cleats just long enough to slip over the flanges of the channels as they rest on the base, and fasten them in place between each pair of frames with one wood screw through the center of each cleat. This will clamp the frames to the base so they do not wiggle around when the press is operated. Two lengths of 1 x 2 lumber, free from knots, are cut to reach from the first to the last frame, and these are screwed to each frame on the top between the press screws. These tie the frames together at the top, and, incidentally, make a convenient place to store the pressure-bars when the press is opened.

For the bed of the press, you will need three lengths of 4-inch I-beam, each 9 feet long, or eight 2 x 4's, straight and true, also 9 feet long. The steel beams are by far the best to use, as they are much more rigid. However, if you use 2 x 4's, one should be put through the inside of the frames tightly against the pipe spacers on each side, two right together in the center of the frames, and pairs centered tightly together on each side of the middle.

You must make sure that the 2 x 4's are all exactly the same width. It would be better to run one edge over the jointer, then rip them all to the same size, taking off just a small amount to leave them as wide as possible.

Three 5 x 9 foot panels of ¾-inch fir plywood are ripped in two down the middle. Three of these narrow panels are slid in the frames nesting on the I-beams or the wooden bars. These form the bottom blanket and are left in place at all times.

Two more of the panels are used as the top blankets, and the last piece is not needed.

Two sheets of hard-rolled aluminum, not less than $\frac{5}{1000}$ inch thick, and 2 feet by 9 feet in size can be obtained from your metal supply company. You should ask for ST-grade, which is the symbol designating hard-drawn or hard-rolled plate stock. Slide one of these plates on top of the bottom blanket and leave it in place permanently.

Next cut nine pieces of 4 x 4 lumber: fir or yellow pine, *not*

Put one screw into each frame. This is enough to hold the frames securely when tightening the press.

Space the bed girders evenly on the bottoms of the frames. Two-by-fours can also be used.

The final setting-up operation is the insertion of the bottom metal blanket. The press is now ready to use.

redwood or cedar. Redwood and cedar are much too soft to use as pressure bars. The bars should be cut 2 feet long, to fit inside the frames.

In use, the press is simplicity itself. The one thing you want to get in the habit of doing is to clean the metal plate just before you start, making certain that no chips of wood or drops of glue are on it. Also make sure that all the press screws are wound open all the way.

After your panel is put in glue, slide it into the press, all the way back. If you are making only a short panel, you should put a filler panel into the press in front of the one you are gluing. The filler panel must be exactly the same thickness as the one you are working.

Slide the second metal sheet on top of the work, and on top of that slide the two plywood blanket panels. Slip a 4 x 4 pressure bar under each row of screws across the width of the press and run all the screws down until snug and tight. Then go over the entire press tightening the center screws first. They should be run down to the limit of your strength, unless you happen to be a circus strong man, that is. After the center row is down, take up on one outside row, then the other outside row. You will now find that the center row is loose, and it must be tightened a second time. Check the outside rows again and take up where necessary.

The main thing to keep in mind is that the pressure on each of the screws should be the same. It is poor practice for two people to run up a press together, since almost invariably one will tighten more or less than the other. Two people can close a press only if the final tightening is done by one person alone. That way you are sure you have even pressure through the entire area.

The glue should run freely out of the edges; using aluminum plates there is no danger of ruining your work. When the glue hardens it will snap cleanly off the metal plates.

A word of caution here is indicated. When the panel is removed from the press the edges on the bottom side will be filled with variously sized round patches of glue squeezed from the panel.

These are as sharp as razors, and if you run your hands across them you can cut your fingers to the bone! You should keep a pair of leather-palmed work gloves handy for use on the press, and always wear them when removing the panels. Then, still wearing the gloves, you can snap off the glue spills before you handle the work.

While it will make the cost a little more than building your own press from the ground up, it is possible to buy frames already made. Many craftsmen who would like to do this work might be unable to make the press because of not having the equipment to build one. The Adjustable Clamp Company can supply frames made up in two sizes, which can be assembled on your base to complete the press in whatever length you want. The ready-made frames will solve that problem very nicely.

Frames can be made out of 4 x 4 lumber if you find it difficult to get or work steel channels.   *Courtesy Adjustable Clamp Company*

5

HOW TO BUILD YOUR
OWN VENEER EDGER

The next most important piece of shop equipment for the veneersman is the edger. Here, again, a commercial edger costs in the neighborhood of eight thousand dollars but you can make one for around fifty dollars that will do a very creditable job. I have used such an edger for several years, and make matches that are absolutely undetectable as far as glue-lines are concerned.

The slightest error in matching the two edges of veneers results in an unsightly glue-line that can never be removed and can only be disguised if you stain the work a color darker than the glue. In my opinion, staining is one of the cardinal sins in veneering. No stains should be used on veneers, because the very reason you use veneers to begin with is to take advantage of the wonderful natural colors, grains, and patterns available. To stain such woods is unthinkable.

A commercial edger is a sturdy machine with a high-speed multiple-edge cutter rotating in a fixed position. A travelling table with a hydraulically operated clamping bar running the length of the table is positioned in front of the cutter. The veneer sheets are placed on the table in a stack equal to the width of the cutter and clamped close to the edge by the clamping bar. The cutter is now started; the table is pushed across the face of the cutter which slices a thin shaving off the stack of veneers. The travel of the table is kept true and straight by precision tracks upon which it runs, and the cutter is mounted rigidly on a heavy arbor. Some edgers have motor-driven tables, so all the workman does is clamp up the stack of veneers and flip the switch.

Our homemade edger performs the same job, though it uses a slightly different system and is manually operated. The table stands still and the cutter moves. A high-speed router forms the business end of our homemade affair, and it is equipped with a special tungsten-carbide cutter. Stanley Tool Company makes a straight-faced cutter for trimming Micarta and Formica counter tops. This is a cutter about ½ inch long, mounted on an arbor with a special ball-bearing race exactly the same diameter as the cutter for a guide. The cutter is faced with tungsten carbide and the cutting edge lasts a very long time.

Two boards 1 foot longer than the press and at least 8 inches wide are needed. These must be absolutely flat and true, and should be of a hard, stable wood. Hard mahogany is excellent for the purpose, or well-dried true and straight walnut will serve admirably, if you can find it. As a last resort, if your lumber yard does not have good hardwoods, you can use a softer wood; cypress would be one of the best because it does not warp readily, comes straight and without defects, and is easily worked. Not all lumber yards stock cypress, however. Redwood is entirely unfit; it splits too easily.

One edge of one board must be joined absolutely straight and true. The accuracy with which this is done determines the accuracy of the edge-joints you have in your veneer panels. If you cannot handle a board as long as this with absolute accuracy, take it to a lumber yard and have them true it up for you. If they true it on a jointer, insist that they feed the board through the machine very slowly to avoid putting ripples on the edge. An even better way of having the edge trued is in a fenceless saw if your lumber yard has one. Almost every good millwork factory has one or more of these machines. In them, the board is fed past a saw blade by rollers and does not run against a fence. These machines are used

44

Rout the rabbet for the angle so the metal surface is exactly flush with the face of the board.

to true up boards which have a bend in them and which are hard to handle on a jointer. It is fast and accurate and the edge as it comes from the saw is fine for our purpose.

A length of angle $\frac{3}{4}$ x $\frac{3}{4}$ x $\frac{1}{8}$ inch thick and as long as the board is required. Brass is best, aluminum next best. Steel angle is not suitable because the surface is not true and smooth enough.

A rabbet is run on the trued edge of the board to allow the angle to be set covering the edge and flush with the face. It must not be lower than flush. At least every 6 inches along the angle, drill and countersink holes for wood screws to fasten the angle in place. These screws are on the face side of the board only, not the edge which must be left smooth and intact. With the angle fastened in place you have completed the edger.

To edge the veneer, the sheets are taped together in stacks of not more than six thicknesses, four if the veneer is sawn instead of sliced. The sheets of veneer should be held with masking tape around each end, but not around the sides, which are going to be cut off when edged.

When stacking veneers to run through the edger, always remember to stack them in the order they are to be used. This order

Drill and countersink the metal angle so the screw heads will be slightly less than flush on the top face of the edging board.

should be maintained until the final operation of taping is completed, or you will be unable to make your matches of grain and color. In matching end grains, always edge the sides first. Then the stack can be put in the edger and positioned accurately with a square set on the guide angle, with the veneer held against the

Screw the angle down about every 6 inches. Hold it tight to the edge of the board with a bar clamp while you are placing the screws.

square blade. Remember that any error in the squareness of your cut is doubled when the veneers are taped together.

Lay the taped veneers on top of the board with the metal angle, with the stack projecting out over the angle about 1/8 inch. Carefully lay the second board with its edge just set back from the metal angle of the lower board a tiny bit. Clamp the entire assembly together with a handscrew at each end, and at least one in the middle. If you are edging veneer the full length of the press, then three clamps should be spaced equally in the center of the edging boards, making five clamps down the length.

Adjust the height of the router cutter so that the cutting edges span the veneer and the ball-bearing guide rests fully on the metal angle. Start at the right-hand end of the board and, resting the router firmly on the top board, the ball-bearing guide held firmly against the metal angle, slowly run the cutter down the board until it touches the first clamp. Lift the router around the clamp

Keep the router firm against the metal edge and down on the top board.

and continue cutting until the next clamp is reached. Repeat the operation until you have travelled the length of the veneer.

Using a spare clamp, fasten it to the assembly on one side or the other of the first clamp on the board, far enough away so the router will cut the edge of the veneer which was not cut on the first pass. Remove the first clamp and use that to replace the next, and so on down the length of the board. Then run the router

47

down the spots left on the first pass. Always run the router very slowly, and be careful to maintain even pressure both *down* on the top board and *in* against the metal angle.

Never remove a clamp to make your second run until you have first put a second clamp next to it. To do so is to invite disaster, since opening the center of the edger assembly gives the veneer a chance to slip imperceptibly. While you may not have noticed the movement, and while it might be only about $\frac{1}{1000}$ inch, it will be enough to ruin the close fit needed in matching.

If the veneer you are working with has a slight warp or curl, it may be possible to clamp it up in the edger without flattening. This can be determined by laying the veneer on a flat surface and placing a flat board on top of it. Then press down on the board, listening carefully at the same time. If you can press the sheet of veneer flat without hearing it snap or pop, you can clamp it into the edger without fear of too much damage. Should you hear a snap when you press it flat, however, you know that somewhere in the sheet a split occurred due to the tight shrinkage. If this happens when you flatten the veneer, it will happen when you clamp it in the edger. If it occurs in the edger one of two things will happen. Either the veneer will spread at the site of the split and will then spring back when you edge the stack and remove it from the clamps, leaving a hollow that cannot be pulled up tightly when taping; or the split will open to allow the veneer to be clamped flat, then close again when the pressure is released, pulling the joint out of alignment.

If the veneer can be flattened without splitting, be careful to stack the sheets exactly in line before clamping. That is, each point on any sheet should be exactly above or below the identical point on the adjacent sheets. This way, all the flattening pressures will be in the same places on each individual sheet and there will be no comparative distortion between the sheets.

Veneers that are free of natural oils often dry out with considerable shrinkage. This causes the sheets to warp and curl. With a complicated grain, this warpage may take the form of waving and curling something like a potato chip. If the veneer you are working with has this property, it must be handled very carefully when it is clamped into the edger. Otherwise it will split or crack, sometimes with a split opening up a considerable way—so far, in fact, that it cannot be brought back together again.

Most of the time, such warped veneers can be flattened by moistening them slightly and clamping them gently between thick newspapers between boards. You cannot actually wet the veneers, or you will have to allow them to dry out again for several weeks. If the veneers are wet when taped up and glued onto a panel, as they dry they will warp the panel and split all over the surface. The amount of tension exerted by drying veneer is little short of amazing. The thin layer of face veneer can pull a heavy plywood panel into a bow by the shrinkage due to drying when improperly wet.

A sponge rung out until it does not drip and rubbed stiffly over the surface of the veneer on both sides generally provides enough moistening to allow the wood to be flattened. If you have only a piece or two to use for the panel you are working on, then the flattening can be done by laying the sheets between newspaper, putting a board on top and standing a few bricks or concrete blocks on the cover board. Any heavy weight would serve, of course.

If there are several thicknesses of veneer to be flattened, this is the best method to follow. Sponge off the first sheet and lay it between layers of newspapers; sponge the next and add it to the stack, covering with newspaper, building up as you go. Pay particular attention to stacking each sheet exactly on top of the preceding one. If the edges overlap or overhang, the sheets will not be under pressure and as they dry, will warp all over again, sometimes so badly that they cannot be saved. When the entire stack has been sponged and papered, it can be slid into the veneer press, a blanket slid on top, and the whole clamped up just enough—but not to gluing pressure—to flatten the veneers. Leave the assembly in the press for two days, then remove it and replace the newspapers with fresh ones. Return the stack to the press for another two or three days, and repeat the process of replacing the newspaper. The third time the stack can be left under slight pressure for four or five days, after which time the moisture should be equalized in the veneers enough to allow you to work them up with little danger of continued shrinkage.

Veneers which have been flattened should be edged up, matched, taped, and put in glue as fast as possible. By that I mean you should not leave them out in the air for days at a time after flattening, or they will simply dry out and warp all over again into their old pattern. The best thing to do is to edge them and put the panel in glue, then stand the panel up in the rack to cure. The veneers should be stable, if you left them in the pressure stack for a long enough time. The work cannot be hastened, and should not be cut short. As I mentioned in my introduction, you are handling precious material. The time you take to work it is well spent, and good insurance that the job is being done the way it should. In all work with veneers, each step should be given the time it needs to do it right. You only get one chance with each batch of veneer, remember.

It is bad practice generally to use veneers of two different thicknesses on the same panel. Sometimes, however, it must be done, either for effect or because a customer wants two particular woods together that are only available in different thicknesses. This would be true when blending ebony with other woods, for instance. Ebony is generally available only as sawn veneer of $\frac{1}{20}$ inch thickness, while the other wood may be sliced to $\frac{1}{28}$ inch thickness.

You will run into trouble trying to glue up a panel of two varying thicknesses, but more about that in another part of this book. (See Chapter 8, pages 83–84) The trouble you will have right now is in edging your work. If you were making a panel of two veneers alternating in straight bands, the thing would be easy enough. You would merely edge each sheet and tape them together. But usually this is not the way veneers would be put together. For instance, a table top being made of two contrasting veneers might have a burl center with ebony dividing bands crossing to make four square panels. If the ebony were carried around the outside edges only, it would be a cinch, since it could be routed in the same way as a panel border. But if the thicker veneer were crossing dividing bands, you would be in trouble, since each pair of adjacent joints would have to be edged together to make a good glue-line. On the long edges it is simple; you stack a thick and a thin veneer and edge them together. But in edging up the joints for a panelled top, each panel in the top has to be edged on all four sides. When you cross from one veneer to the other, you will almost invariably split out the joint where the two different thicknesses come together. This trouble can be alleviated somewhat by building up the thickness of the thinner veneer with tape along the edges which are to be clamped and edged with the router for the joint. This makes it difficult to match the veneers after edging, and when you tape them, you have hidden the veneer with the tape. Also, this built-up edge will merely transfer the point of pressure when the panel is finally assembled in the press. So, while you licked your problem in the edger, you created another in the veneer press.

Another way the work can be clamped in the edger is to use strips of paper to build up to the same thickness as the heavier veneer. Add the paper strips one at a time, measuring the pile with a micrometer as you go until it is within a couple of thousandths of an inch of the thicker veneer. Then tape the pile together to hold it while it is in the edger. Still a third way, and one I use frequently, is to use masking tape to build up the thickness of the thinner veneer, edging the veneer, tape and all. While this is somewhat messy at times, as the gum on the tape may clog the cutter, still the convenience of having everything held together while you work is worth the extra trouble of cleaning the cutter with lacquer-thinner after each pass across the tape. After the edges have been trued up, the remaining tape can be carefully peeled from the veneer, leaving it exposed so you can match up the joints.

Your edger boards should be stored in such a manner that air can freely circulate around them. They should never be laid down on a solid surface except when they are in use, and then, when you have finished the job at hand, should be stacked separately again. This is to minimize the possibility of warping, which even in a slight degree, would be enough to throw out the precision of the edge cut. The top of the veneer press is a good place to store the edger boards, since they rest upon the press screws and the air can circulate all about them. Be sure that they are supported for their entire length, however, or you will introduce a warp in them that is due to mechanical distortion rather than shrinkage.

6

CORES AND CORE STOCK

The center or core is a most important part of a panel. Although never seen, if not properly constructed it will warp or delaminate and ruin all the work that went into building the furniture made from it.

Plywood core is excellent for furniture-making and, in fact, is generally the only type of core I use in making up my own panels. However, there are times when a commercial panel is used for the face because some particularly desirable kind of veneer is available at the time. When this is the case you will most often find that lumber core is used for making the plywood. Poplar, chestnut, and basswood are the most frequently used woods. All of these have several features in common: they glue easily and well; they dry thoroughly so the core may be stabilized against warping; they are always readily available; and they are cheap. Lauan, which is often sold under the name of Philippine mahogany, is also excellent core material. It is not a mahogany, however, and should not be so called. Lauan is a fibrous wood, very like poplar but with a more open grain, and it glues well.

Lumber warps because the water in the cells evaporates unequally, causing a correspondingly uneven shrinkage along the cell lines. A cross-sectional view of a tree will show circular annular rings. These rings are rows of cells which carry the sap in the tree. A board cut from the tree near the bark will have longer portions of these rings in it than one cut nearer the heart. From face to face in the board the rings will differ in length, causing the board to pull toward the outer side or back side as it dries, if left to dry without some kind of control.

To minimize warpage, lumber is dried in huge ovens, or kilns, until the moisture content is lowered to the point of stabilization with the surrounding air. If the lumber is then stacked so the air can circulate freely around all surfaces, it will remain flat and straight indefinitely. If, however, the boards are indiscriminately piled on top of each other, they will dry out their exposed sides, with shrinkage occuring as they dry, causing the board to curl up at the ends.

Wide boards have a tendency to warp more quickly than narrow ones, because there are more lines of cells to give up water in a wide surface. For this reason it is always best to build up a core panel out of narrow strips rather than from one or two wide boards. The boards to be used in the core may be ripped into 2- or 3-inch strips, then glued up into the wide panel, reversing each alternate strip so the grain changes direction. In other words, the heartwood side of one board should be alternated with the bark-wood side of the neighboring strip. The heartwood side can easily be determined by looking at the end of the board. The rings will show a curve, slight or strong, depending on the diameter and section of the tree from which the board was cut. The hollow, or concave side of the rings is the heart side of the board. An easy method of keeping the sides known is to draw a line across the width of the board on one side before ripping it into strips. Then reverse every other strip when you glue up, without paying any attention to which is heart side or which is bark side.

The edges of the strips must be planed smooth and straight before gluing. If this operation is done by hand, two strips should be planed together with their marked surfaces outermost when clamped in the vise. The edges must be square and true. There may be a slight hollow in the center of each strip but on no account can it be high. A hollow will be pulled up tightly by the clamps but a high spot will cause the strips to snap apart at the ends after the glue has set. As each pair of edges is fitted, they should be marked so you will be able to keep track of them. A different pencil mark on the edges of each pair is enough to go by. When all the strips are fitted, they can be glued up into the panel using three bar clamps. One should be placed at each end of the panel on the same side, and the third positioned in the center of the opposite side. This will equalize the pressure and not introduce a warp in the panel while the glue is setting.

If you are making several cores of the same size, it would be easier to clamp them all in one operation, using either piling clamps or the homemade stacking clamps described in the chapter on clamps and clamping.

After the panel has set, the surface may be sanded smooth and true. Any bend or twist must be planed flat and all glue must be cleaned from the two sides before it can be used as a core. The most convenient thickness of finished panels for furniture work is 3/4 inch. The core stock should be made up to 5/8 inch thick to allow for two layers of crossbanding and two layers of face veneer. As core panels are finished they should be stored standing vertically in a rack that allows the air to circulate freely around them. Several core panels may be made at one time and stocked for future use.

The alternate core stock is plywood, and I use this material to the exclusion of anything else, except for chip or flake board for tops of cabinets which do not require joint stress.

Plywood can be purchased exactly 5/8 inch thick, good one side or good both sides. This thickness makes up into a good 3/4-inch finished panel after crossbanding and face veneers have been added. That grade which is good one side is fine for most work, especially cabinets where one face of the finished panel is inside out of sight. The few knots and depressions left on the bad face may be filled with surfacing putty, plastic wood, or any other kind of filler that hardens quickly, then sanded smooth before crossbanding.

When surfacing putty is used in repairing the core prior to

crossbanding, unless the putty is thoroughly mixed and has enough solvent in it to make it soft and sticky, the entire repair can, after a time, loosen and lift off the panel. If the panel has been crossbanded and veneered before this happens, the loosening of the patch can cause a lot of trouble.

Chip or flake board is sold under many trade names but all of them are pretty much the same. They are smooth and vary in thickness, and make excellent gluing surfaces. They are made out of chips of woods impregnated with a binder and compressed into panels. They have no shear strength to speak of, and a wide panel of flake board may be cracked in half over your knee. They also will not hold screws or nails well. Their value lies in their smooth surfaces and their weight. Chip or flake board is ideal for tops of tables, chests, and cabinets, but unsuitable for doors or lids where hinges would have to be mounted, since they have very little holding strength.

Whatever material you use for the core of a veneered panel, great care and discrimination should be exercised in selecting it, since this is the foundation upon which you are building your work, and the work will be no better than the foundation. The fact that the core will never be seen after the work is finished is not a reason for skimping in any way on the quality or exactness of it. The grades of plywood that are sold in the lumber yards under the names of plyscored and sheathing grade plywood are not suitable for veneering core stock. They are roughly made, with little attention paid to the tightness of the glue-lines, and often inferior grade veneer is used in the manufacture of such panels. For the purpose for which they were designed, they are excellent. As sheathing on the sidewalls of a house to be covered with brick or other siding, for the underlayment of a sub-floor or the sub-roofing, they are exactly what is needed. For veneering panels for use in the manufacture of fine furniture, they are unsuitable. Only slightly better is the plywood sold under the grading "touched one side." This is a plyscored or sheathing panel that has been lightly sanded on the "good" side, which side is not very good to begin with as far as our requirements are concerned.

What we need for core stock is standard interior or exterior grade plywood, sanded both sides. It should be good one side if it is to be used for panels that will have one side unexposed, or good both sides if the completed work is a door on a cabinet or otherwise open to view on both sides after veneering.

With the core panels made up we are ready to turn our attention to the crossbanding. This is the inner layer of veneer laid at right angles to the core and just under the face and back veneers in a ¾-inch thick panel. In thicker panels made up of plywood core there may be several layers of crossbanding.

Poplar is generally used for crossbanding because of its low cost and availability, and the fact that it is rotary-sliced, hence obtainable in very wide widths. However, mahogany is the best wood to use for crossbands, especially the last layer directly underneath the face and back veneer. Poplar could be used in the inner layers if desired.

Here, again, we should realize that, while it will never be seen, the crossbanding is a most important part of a veneered panel. For the final crossbanding right under the face veneer, good quality, clear, wide mahogany should be used. This glues better than most other woods, but the real reason is that there is no grain to telegraph through to the surface when the face veneer is applied. Crossbanding with knots or holes may be filled and used, but there is an excellent chance of the defect being seen when the face veneer is sanded after laying up the panel. It is better to confine your use of such second quality stock to the side of the panel that will be inside a cabinet, or which will not be seen after construction. A second factor in the choice of mahogany for crossbanding over other woods—poplar or whitewood, for instance—is the greater dimensional stability of mahogany, which makes it less likely to shrink after fabrication, causing warpage.

The crossbanding is cut with the grain running across the grain of the core panel. If your crossbanding veneer is not wide enough to cover the entire core then it must be joined together in the same fashion as the face veneer, but in this case extreme care in jointing is not necessary. You are not attempting to match grain or pattern, but merely to increase width. Since the crossbanding is going to end up glued inside the panel, it does not matter if very small openings occur in the seams, because the glue will fill them when the final layer is glued in place. Under no circumstance do I mean to imply that you should or could make a poor joint in crossbanding, depending on the glue to cover the shoddy workmanship. What I do mean is that, when taping crossband veneers, if you can see light through a part of the joint, it can be glued up anyway, since the great pressure in the veneer press would expel glue through the opening and fill it. By "very small opening" I mean an opening less than the thickness of the page these words are printed on, no more.

The sheets of crossbanding veneer may be taped together with short lengths of paper masking tape placed on the outside face. This tape can be pulled off after the panel comes out of the press, since it does not matter too much if the grain is slightly fuzzy from the removal of the tape. Make up two sheets of crossbanding about an inch larger than the core panel. This in turn should be an inch or two larger than the finished panel size.

Gluing the panels demands that you develop a system to suit your individual working characteristics, one that should become routine to avoid possible errors. First you will need a solid flat area on which to work when gluing. An old door set across two horses makes an excellent worktable, provided it is one of the flush variety, not one with indented panels. Tape up the two crossband panels of veneer ready for gluing and put one aside. On the other, on the tape side of the veneer, stick short lengths of masking tape on each end and one or more on each side. These lengths should not be longer than 3 or 4 inches and should be attached so as to project a couple of inches beyond the veneer. Lay this sheet of crossbanding on the table with the taped side *down*, then position the core panel on top of it.

There are several methods of applying the glue to large panels. Certain paint rollers have sleeves that slip off the roller. If you can find one of these, remove the sleeve, then glue a sheet of thin foam rubber, cork, or heavy canvas around the roller, using Weldwood glue mixed to the same proportions as for veneering. To insure a tight joint, hold the foam or other fabric in place with a few turns of masking tape while the glue is curing. Foam fabric comes in sheets about $\frac{1}{16}$ inch thick; both outsides are pebbled foam rubber and the inside is strong cloth weave. If none of these materials is available to you, then the shortest nap roller you can find will do. Or you may use a stiff wide brush, although brushing glue on a large panel is a real chore and, unless you are really hopping, may take too long. The working time from the start of spreading the glue to closing the press is about fifteen minutes. Apply the glue to the top surface of the core panel; then turn the panel over and place it glue side down on top of the crossbanding. Apply glue to the second side of the core and lay the second sheet of crossbanding on the glued surface with the taped side *up*. Bind the sandwich together with the short pieces of masking tape brought around the edges and stuck to the top crossband sheet. Lift the entire sandwich and slide it into the press, keeping the end toward you raised until the entire panel is slid far enough into the press. Close the press and leave the panel in it overnight to set the glue.

If your press has three rows of screws, always run the center row down snug first, working right down the press. Make no attempt to run these up tight; just snug them enough to put the panel under pressure. This will keep the glue-line from drying out. Now you can run down the two outer rows of screws; tighten each row as much as you can, and then go back to tighten the center row.

After curing in the press, the panel is removed and the tape pulled from the joints. A very light sanding can be given the surface if desired, especially if the tape pulled any of the grain when removed. Panels should be equalized for a day after gluing unless the face veneer is ready to apply and the finished work returned to the press immediately. Equalizing means that the panel is stood on end, vertically, held upright either in a rack or by leaning against a corner of an object that permits air to circulate about either face. Never lay a panel down on a flat surface, especially not just after removing from the press. When it is still damp from the water in the glue, it will warp beyond reclaim in a very short time.

The edges should not be trimmed on crossbanded panels, but left with the overhang until the face veneers have been applied. This will protect the panel and insure that the crossbanding is not snapped off beyond the finished edge. Keep track of the side with the repairs. Mark this side so you will be able to recognize it when, after the crossbanded panel is removed from the press, you are ready for the face and back veneers. The repaired side of the core should always be the side that is back veneered so it will be on the inside of the cabinet made from the panel, where any uneveness or inequalities will go unnoticed. Also, it is possible, though not probable, that the repaired places may loosen in time. Inside the article of furniture this is immaterial, but if it happened under the face veneer the piece would be ruined.

7

MATCHING VENEERS

Veneers are put together edge to edge, for several reasons. The first and most common reason for doing so is to make a wide panel out of narrow pieces of veneer. Many veneers are available only in very narrow strips, and in order to take advantage of their beauty, grain, or figure, they must be grouped together to form a usable width. If the veneer were glued in haphazard order, the constant and abrupt changing of grain and pattern would be most unsightly and disturbing. It takes careful matching, therefore, to create an object of beauty out of these narrow strips; the greatest amount of time and care should be exercised to make the best match, since it is here that the craftsman can bring all his ingenuity into play to produce panels of rare beauty and value.

Sometimes veneers are matched to produce figures and patterns not normal to the wood as it grows, but which, when carefully put together, make an overall pattern that is far more attractive than the natural figure and grain. Burls, crotches, and stump veneers are often treated in this fashion.

Whatever the purpose, the methods of matching different sections are much the same. Many veneers have a grain so wild and ungovernable that it is next to impossible to match each line or figure. Some veneers, as in the case of highly-figured tamo, are cut from the flitch at such an angle that the grain changes radically within the thickness of the veneer sheet, making it very difficult to bring two edges into perfect match.

61

The idea in matching is to take two sheets of veneer—adjacent in the flitch and in the order in which it was sliced—and to position them edge to edge in such fashion that each line, figure, color, etc., is in perfect juxtaposition with the matching sheet. This, when glued up on the core, and when the glue-line is so tight that it does not show, produces a panel on which the veneer offers a pattern symmetrical around the matching line. In plainer grains, straight-figured woods, and solid color woods this is a simple matter. Simply stack the sheets of veneer in the order to be glued, edge them, tape them, and lay up the panel. In highly figured veneers and veneers cut to such an acute angle that the pattern changes abruptly—as with tamo—great care must be taken. The sheets should be played with, moved from one position to another, slid up or down next to each other until the most accurate continuance of line is obtained. Then the sheets should be taped for edging in this position, and marked in some fashion so they can be repositioned after edging when assembled for taping.

In the case of many commercial veneer panels, the pieces of veneer are taken from the flitch with little or no regard for the careful matching of grain, edged, taped together, and glued up. The idea here is to produce panels wide enough to work with, faced with a good veneer for overall color or grain, but with no attention paid to the figures obtainable by matching.

The more usual case is that the individual slices of veneer are somewhat cursorially matched, in an attempt to make some kind of homogeneous pattern. The next stage in commercial veneered panel production is to actually try for good matching *within the stock possibilities of the flitch*. That is, two adjacent strips of veneer are moved up or down in relation to each other enough to make a match of the major part of the grain and figure with the least amount of waste from discarded lengths of the strips. To find

The four-way-center-and-butt is usually called quarter-matching. Here are several variations of this style of matching.

DIFFERENT WAYS OF MATCHING VENEERS

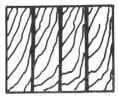

BOOK MATCH

All types of veneers are used. In book matching, every other sheet is turned over just as are the leaves of a book. Thus, the back of one veneer meets the front of the adjacent veneer, producing a matching joint design.

SLIP MATCH

In slip matching, veneer sheets are joined side by side and convey a sense of repeating the flitch figure. All types of veneer may be used, but this type of matching is most common in quarter-sliced veneers.

VERTICAL BUTT AND HORIZONTAL BOOKLEAF MATCH

Where the height of a flitch does not permit its fabrication into the desired height of panel, it may be matched vertically as well as horizontally.

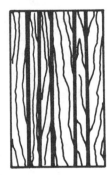

RANDOM MATCH

Veneers are joined with the intention of creating a casual unmatched effect. Veneers from several logs may be used in the manufacture of a set of panels.

SPECIAL MATCHING EFFECTS

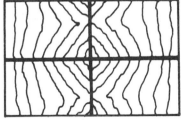

DIAMOND

REVERSE DIAMOND

FOUR-WAY CENTER AND BUTT

This type of match is ordinarily applied to Butt, Crotch or Stump veneers, since it is the most effective way of revealing the beauty of their configurations. Occasionally flat cut veneers are matched in this manner where panel length requirements exceed the length of available veneers.

"V"

HERRINGBONE

perfect grain matches often creates too much waste to be commercially economical.

This is where the individual craftsman has the edge on the commercial manufacturer. First of all, he is doing the work either for himself or for a custom order. He can take more pains to make a perfect match. While he might waste a lot more veneer, relatively, than the commercial man, the end result is probably so much better that it justifies the waste. And while the individual may pay more per square foot for the smaller quantities of veneer he buys, he can charge more for the finished panel. Certainly a panel made to specifications out of top quality veneer and with more time and care spent in the matching is worth more than a panel bought out of stock from a comercial press company.

Oftentimes a veneer, especially a butt, stump, or burl, has such a pattern that it is useless as panel material. Perhaps the grain is a stripe which runs diagonally off the piece from one corner to the other. To try to make a panel out of this kind of veneer that will look well made up into furniture is very difficult, since there is very little aesthetic value in such a pattern. This type of figure is, however, excellent for matching up into a larger panel. It is perfect for diamond-pattern matching, cross-pattern matching, or herringbone matching and is often found in French walnut veneers.

Burls often have distinct pattern designs, although the great majority of burls are more or less evenly patterned swirls, knots, eyes, and rings. When a burl is so large that it can be used as the entire center portion of a framed panel, for instance, no attention has to be placed on the figure; the purpose of using the burl in the first place is as a center pattern of whatever figure is normal to that burl. When the burl is mixed with "long-wood" grain, however, as in the case of Carpathian elm burl, then you have uncommonly good matching possibilities, and can sometimes make up panels that are absolutely beautiful, and so rare they are almost one-in-a-lifetime productions. Here every advantage can be taken of the long grain for the match lines, leaving the burl for the fancy

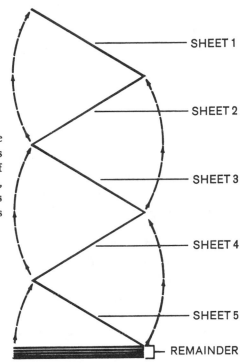

Sheets are "accordioned" off the stack so that alternate edges touch. Always keep the points of the "Vees" together. Sheets 1, 3, and 5 will be turned over; sheets 2 and 4 will remain facing as they were in the stack.

SHEET 1

SHEET 2

SHEET 3

SHEET 4

SHEET 5

REMAINDER

figure. Since long grain is far easier to match than burl grains, the panels very often look as though they are made from one piece.

There are several ways to match veneers to make up panels wider than the individual sheets. Perhaps the most often used method is *book-matching*. In this method all kinds of veneers are used, even burls. In practice, every other sheet is turned over as you would turn the pages of a book, Thus, the back of one veneer meets the front of the adjacent sheet, producing a matched design at the joint.

When a panel is book-matched, the grain of every alternate strip of veneer reverses itself. Thus, if the first strip shows highlights in one or more areas, the next strip will have dark color or non-reflecting grain in the same area. The third strip will be as the first, the fourth strip as the second, and so on for the entire width of the panel. Often, in business buildings, banks, and other public places, an entire flitch will be made up into panels to run consecutively clear around the room. When this is done, the effect is very interesting. The panels are carefully marked as they are laid up, and each panel is veneered in a continuation of the way the sheets lie in the flitch. Thus starting in one corner of the room, the pattern continues to match all around the four walls.

Sometimes the doors are set into one of the panels, veneered exactly the same as the panel in such a fashion that, except for the hardware and the frame line, the door itself is all but invisible. In book-matching, the effect is that of taking the individual sheets of veneer off the flitch in the manner of an accordion door, or a pleated piece of paper. Each sheet is joined to the preceding one on its alternate edge. That is to say, if you place the flitch down on a bench before you, the top and second sheets would be edged on their left sides. The second and third sheets edged on their right sides, the third and fourth sheets on the left again, and so on down through the flitch. This means that the first two sheets are opened as the pages of a book. Then, assuming that the two sheets have already been attached to each other, treat them as though they were one sheet and lift them open from the stack to the opposite direction, repeating this performance each time you match up two sheets. This places the top of one sheet and the bottom of the next sheet on the same plane, alternating through the stack. Reference to the sketch will make the method of book-matching perfectly plain.

To obtain the most regular pattern in book-matching, the stack of veneer should be squared up to the width of the narrowest sheet. As the sheets run down into the flitch, they become wider. This is understandable, because the tree increases in girth toward the center of the trunk. The pattern remains true in the same parts of all the sheets, so it would be impossible to accurately match a wide sheet with a narrow one. The stack should therefore be cut to the width of the top or narrowest sheet before any match-

NARROWEST SHEET IN THE FLITCH.

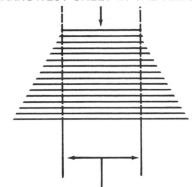

Make certain that the sheets are stacked so that the pattern of the grain is exactly in register with the sheets on top and below, before trimming to the narrowest width.

TRIM TO THIS WIDTH, AND SAVE THE TRIMMINGS FOR EDGE VENEERING OR BORDERING.

ing is done, or before the sheets are edged. If there is a great difference in the widths of the sheets, as is sometimes the case, so much the better; the trimmings will be wide enough for use as edge veneers or border veneers in framed panels.

Slip-matching is most often used with quarter-sliced veneers, although any kind of veneer can be used. Here the sheets of veneer are slid off the flitch side by side. The result is an endlessly repetitive pattern of equal width.

Sometimes consecutive panels for continuous walls of an office or room are slip- or random-matched, instead of book-matched. This is often done with veneers which have a boisterous figure, but no definite pattern. Tigerwood, bubinga, paldao are some of the veneers that can be treated this way. Slip-matching has the advantage of keeping the highlights all on the same side of the veneer, and with veneers having strong highlights in the grain, this can sometimes be very dramatic in effect, because, whatever way you view this wall, the highlights cover it entirely instead of in stripes. Of course, when you move to the opposite side of the

For slip-matching veneer, always slip the sheets off the stack in the same direction, in order to maintain repetition of the pattern.

room to view the wall, it is dull, since all the highlights are effective from one aspect only.

If you intend to make a series of wall panels for a room, considerable attention should be paid to the main point-of-view within the finished room. In other words, you should determine just where you will be in the room most of the time. If it is a den, then you would want the best view from your easy chair, or from the fireplace seat. If an office, then the best view should be presented to you when you are seated at your desk. With this fact in mind, the veneers should be matched on the panels with the side up that will give you the greatest reflection of highlights when viewed from your point of vantage. Since each slice of veneer in the flitch will reflect the highlights from the same side, you should pay attention to the way you start matching the sheets. Look at one sheet from first one side and then the other. If the highlights are not too distinct, then wetting the sheet of veneer with lacquer-thinner will make the grain and the highlights pop right out at you. When you have determined which way affords the greatest reflections, start to match up the panels, marking them so they will be installed in the room from one side or the other, as the case may be.

Random-matching creates a casual, unmatched effect, and if the sheets of veneer are edged to different widths, and sheets from different flitches are used, the effect is that of a panel made of regular lumber.

Random-matching is the cheapest, or rather, the most economical way (there is a difference) of making a number of panels. When a room is done in random-matched panelling it has a completely casual appearance, looking as though it had been walled with odd boards of lumber.

Random-matching is economical because each sheet is used in the full width; the difference in widths of the different sheets merely adds to the casual appearance of the panels. The waste that occurs in book-matching is avoided here. Random-matching is fine for wall coverings in certain types of rooms, but in panels intended for use in fine furniture, it has not as much appeal as other kinds of pattern creation.

Herringbone-matching is used with veneers having a more or less straight grain and the figure running diagonally across the sheet. The grain is reversed on each adjacent sheet across the panel, giving the effect of zigzag lines.

Herringbone-matching is also done with veneers having perfectly straight or nearly straight figures running the length of the strip. Zebra wood, sapele, and some of the mahoganies often have striped figures so regular as to appear drawn on the veneer instead of growing in it. Sapele particularly is easily obtained with either fine or wide striping and is much used for vertical bordering on fine tables. The wood is so close to mahogany in color and grain that it is used together with mahogany, and it is hard for the layman to tell that two different woods were used.

When herringbone-matching is done with these straight-grained woods, they are generally matched up to obtain wide sheets first. The matched sheet is treated as though it were one piece, and is cut on the diagonal to obtain the desired angle for the herringbone. In the case of sepele this is easy to do, because the veneer comes flat and true. Rarely is there any warp in this useful veneer. Zebra wood, on the other hand, especially if it has stood for a long time in the veneer house, dries out so badly that it warps, curls, and splits. It splits at the slightest bit of rough handling, too. Perhaps the best way to handle this veneer if you want to herringbone-match it is to dampen it with a solution of glycerine and water in the proportion of 3 ounces of glycerine to 1 gallon of water. Sponge both sides of the veneer and let the moisture soak in for a few minutes; then put it under light pressure overnight, before edging and taping.

Herringbone patterns are made with the taped narrow widths as they fall in the flitch. That is to say, when assembling a number of narrow widths to obtain the desired wide sheet, you may edge each pair of adjacent sheets without bothering to try to match them, since the very pattern of stripes is a match in itself. However, each pair of sheets used for the matching of the herringbone must be very accurately taped. Each narrow strip within the pair of wide sheets must be exactly the same width, or you will be unable to make a herringbone and have the lines come together in a match.

Next, when cutting the angle for the herringbone-match, you must pay particular attention to keeping the cut edges together, since they are the only edges which will make an accurate match. As the angle is cut, one part of the sheet is reversed and the two cut edges brought together again for matching. The top and the bottom of the matched piece will have to be trimmed off to square up the work. Herringbone-matching is not exactly economical, but since the striped veneers are generally low in price compared with the highly-figured ones, it is not beyond the economic possibility of the average veneersman. Where this type of matching shows to best advantage is in paired doors on cabinets. Here, each door is one half of the herringbone, and when both doors are closed, the pattern is complete. On this type of door, the matching edges are not framed; instead, both doors are framed as though they were one single panel.

Vee-matching is the same as herringbone-matching, except that only two sheets are used, with the joint running down the center of the panel.

Quarter-matching yields a great number of fancy patterns. There are several kinds of quarter-matching, the four-way-center-and-butt match being perhaps the most commonly used. This is the most effective way of revealing the beauty of the configurations of butt, crotch, and stump veneers. Occasionally flat-cut veneers are four-way-center-and-butt matched, if the veneer is short and a long panel is required. Another way of gaining length in panels is to match bookleaf horizontally and butt vertically.

Circles, ovals, odd shapes in patterns are obtainable by quarter-matching. French walnut lends itself very well to this kind of pattern matching, since often the grain is composed of alternating light and dark stripes which curve across the width of the sheet. Careful cutting and matching can produce some bizarre and beautiful effects.

Quarter-matching is commonly used for table tops, with an inlay strip separating the quarter-matched center from the border veneer. Almost any figured veneer is good for quarter-matching. This kind of matching is excellent for using up short stock which otherwise would be useless. For this reason it is always good practice, when cutting stacks of veneers to length for making your panels, to save and renumber the short ends and put them in stock against the time you might want to quarter-match some tabletop panels.

Diamond-matching is a variation of quarter-matching which can be used to advantage when the veneer is straight grained with not too much figure. The sheets are cut on an angle and quarter-matched to produce a diamond figure. Reverse diamond-matching is the same principle applied to the same kinds of veneers, but with the grain matched to produce an "X" pattern rather than a closed diamond.

In matching up panels for small tables, cocktail tables, TV tables, and other kinds of tables in sets, you must be careful to use the same part of the sheet for matching each table top. If, for instance, you were making six table tops and they were to be used as a set, you would need four sheets of veneer for each top, or twenty-four sheets in all. It is good insurance to always consider one extra setup when making up sets of panels with the same figures. That would indicate 28 sheets of veneer in all. The sheets are stacked as they come from the flitch, and the best end selected for cutting for this matching. If the panels are to be 24 inches long, 13 inches should be cut off the sheets. Then the butt part of the match is made, the total length of the face veneer would become 26 inches which is plenty for the spare. The thing to remember is that you cannot cut off consecutive lengths of 13 inches all the way down the sheet to match them up for your panels, because if this were done, each table would have a different pattern after matching. The same 13-inch length should be cut off all the sheets in the entire stack, leaving your bundle of veneer sheets that much shorter. Since most sheets of veneer are much longer than you ever use for a panel anyway, taking off short sections for quarter-matching does not necessarily mean that the remainder is wasted.

When sets of panels are made up in this way, each panel will have a figure so close to the preceding one that they will all appear to be identical. Only if all the tops are laid out together can the slight change in pattern be noted. Another thing to remember, when making up such sets is that if care and time are spent in cutting the veneers and matching them, the set takes on the rich appearance of something that has been thought out and made without concern for the amounts of material used. To the layman a piece of veneer cut from a sheet seems to preclude the further use of that sheet; they look upon matched panels as being very rare and costly to make. Actually, they are not, but they do give that impression, which can be used to great advantage when you come to sell such work. Even for your own use, carefully matched identical panels are much nicer than random patterns in the same set of tables.

The other way to make panels for sets of tables is to use different woods with different patterns to begin with. Here you can use the small ends of various veneers—beautifully grained, patterned, or colored—and by quarter-matching can make table panels each one handsome by itself. The set can then be tied together by using the same border on all. Or you can make no attempt to match them and use different borders as well as different center panels. Noble woods will go together without clashing or looking garish, this is to say, in different pieces of furniture. The use of several kinds of veneers in the same piece becomes gaudy and often ostentatious. In a living room full of furniture, however, if each piece is made from a "noble" veneer, every item can be of a different species of veneer with no detrimental effect to any of the pieces.

Rarely will the worker find a veneer in which the grain is so even and true that every single point will come into adjacent position when the sheets are matched. The best thing to do is to determine what part of the grain is the most dominant, and then match that part, allowing the remainder to fall as it will. Generally, the dominant figure will lead the eye away from the mismatched areas so well that only by close scrutiny will the observer be able to detect the lack of absolute match.

Often you will find some odd pieces of veneer which are so beautiful you would like to make them up. However, the possibility of matching odd pieces to make a panel large enough to work with is impossible. Such pieces can sometimes be used to advantage by blocking or panelling them, with dividing or accent strips separating the four body pieces from each other. In this way, matching is not so important because the separation of the areas is large enough to break the visual line between the patterns. As far as possible, of course, you should position the body pieces with a view to having the color, pattern, or grain all point to a common center. However, exact matching is not at all necessary here. The advantage of this style of panel is that it permits the use of burls and stump veneers, which many times are available only as a few ödd sheets, rather than a large flitch of consecutively patterned pieces.

The illustration of a panelled table top shows the easiest sequence to follow when edging the different pieces of veneer. After edging joints 1-1 and 2-2 on pieces E, F, and G, the three pieces are taped together to form one half of the face veneer panel. The edges 3-3 and 4-4 on pieces A, B, and C are edged and taped in the same manner. With the taped assembly handled as one sheet of veneer, it is edged with the center cross strip D at joint 5-5. The

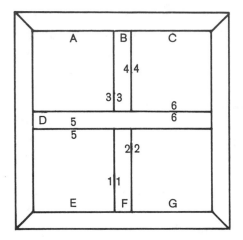

Edging sequence for blocked quarter-matching: E and F are edged at joint 1-1 and the joint taped; F and G are then edged at joint 2-2 and taped. A, B, and C are treated the same, then each assembly is edged to strip D at joints 5-5 and 6-6, and taped as you go. The border is routed on the panel after the matched veneers are glued up.

cross strip is now reversed and edged with the second assembly of pieces A, B, and C.

The point where you can run into trouble is at joints 5-5 and 6-6. With the center strips already taped in the middle of each half-section, any deviation from exactly square will throw the whole panel off square. For this reason you should take extra pains to make certain that the half-panel is placed in the edging clamp with the center strip exactly square to the metal guide edge of the edger. Tape it to the edger board after squaring up the center strip, and lay strip D carefully on top, taping this to the first piece.

The next pitfall you will encounter is edging the second side of strip D with the second half-panel. Here, besides having to insure that the half-panel is perfectly square with the guide edge, you must be certain that strip D is held parallel to its finished edge, or it will come out wedge-shaped, ruining it for assembly.

Perhaps the best way to make sure this strip is parallel is to measure its width very carefully and mark it with a sharp hard pencil after edging the first side. A mark placed at each extreme end will help you position the strip in the edger. In this case, it would be better to put the strip in the edger first, matching the marks with the metal guiding edge, and then tape it firmly in place. The half-panel assembly may then be taped into position, squared up on top of the center strip D, and in turn, taped to the edging board. Be careful when putting the top board in place that you do not shift the work. Do not depend entirely on the tape to hold the work securely. While it should, and even may, be firm enough to take the friction of shifting the top board around to place it accurately, still there is always the chance that the tape will stretch or loosen enough to allow shifting, and the entire work would be ruined. Especially on oily veneers, such as ebony, teak, rosewood, and cypress, is loosening apt to occur. The tape can and often does actually lift up from the veneer though it may have been stuck down securely. This is another reason why it is always best to use gummed paper for taping oily veneers.

Veneers should always be edged in the exact position they are to be matched. The sheets should be cut to the same length after determining the best matching position, then placed in a final exact matching position and marked so they may be returned to this point after edging. You will generally find that the stack of sheets of veneers as you buy them from the factory have some slight imperfection that will act as an excellent guide for positioning the sheets for edging and matching. Perhaps it is a slight curl in the sheets. If so, the curl will be in the same place in each sheet down through the stack and this can be utilized as an index position. Sometimes small knots or even large ones are present. These do not always go through the entire flitch, but they do go part way, and the twisted grain always accompanying the knots will go farther into the tree.

Knots are always welcome when they are intact and tight. They make most interesting figures around a focal point in a panel, and it is a good idea to work around a knot as the point of main interest when it is possible. Often a knot is at the edge of the veneer sheets. When this is the case, you can with great care match the adjacent sheets with the knot in the middle of the match line, sometimes resulting in a wonderfully wild figure. All kinds of imaginary patterns can be read into matched knots—faces, animals, trees, scenes of all kinds. The judicious placement of a good knot can enhance the panel greatly.

Indeed, knots are so valuable a part of the configuration of certain veneers that I always go through as much stock as I can, when buying, to try to find good knots. Perhaps the easiest way to keep track of the matching position when stacking the veneers for edging and subsequent taping is to slide them carefully off one another for an inch or so, trying not to disturb the axial position of the sheets in relation to each other. A dark line carefully drawn across all the exposed edges, at right angles to the edges of the sheets will mark the relative position of all the sheets. If you number all the sheets in a flitch as soon as you get it, you may with impunity remove individual sheets from the stack to examine or repair flaws, knowing that it is an easy matter to return them to the original position. After all positioning is completed, the stack can be taped for edging. Taped veneers should not be kept too long before gluing up into panels. The veneers are apt to warp, split, or become otherwise damaged if they are stored as large taped sheets. A good habit to get into is to always have the core stock ready and crossbanded before starting to match and tape face and back veneers. Then, as soon as it has been taped, the finished panel can be run into the press.

Often, when matching up a pattern in veneers it is difficult to visualize just how the finished piece is going to look. Or you might want to make a diamond- or herringbone-match, but do not know which angle of matching will look best in the panel. Sometimes you have a particularly ornate knot to play with, but the exact position in which to match it cannot be clearly determined. It is often impossible to put two sheets together to see the finished pattern, because the figure you want particularly to match is in the inner portion of the sheet, and, without cutting one sheet or another, you cannot bring the two parts into position.

This difficulty can be overcome by the use of a hinged mirror. Two pieces of plywood from 3 to 6 inches wide and from 8 inches to 1½ feet long are hinged together at one end. Two pieces of

The angle of the mirrors will determine the pattern obtainable. The matching line will be right at the base of the glass.

shock mirror are then fastened to the faces of the plywood. Shock mirror is cheap mirror made on ordinary window glass instead of polished plate. By taking one piece of veneer and placing the folding mirrors on top ot it, you can, by moving the mirrors about, or by changing the angle to which they are folded, easily work out the correct cutting angle for the veneers.

Often a veneer is so brittle that it is difficult to work. This brittleness may be due to the fact that the veneer has dried out too much, or to an inherent quality of that particular type of veneer. Burls are especially prone to brittleness, because their grain is so wild and unpredictable that it runs every which way in the sheet, more often than not being end grain which has no strength at all. Thuya burls, amboyna burls, and Inca burls are the worst offenders in this respect.

In order to work the veneers, edge them, and size them without having them disintegrate in your hands, they should be made more flexible. Wetting them is not enough, nor is it good practice. Instead, they can be treated with a solution which will impart strength to the veneer and, at the same time, "flexibilize" it to the point where it can easily be handled without cracking up into fragments. The solution should be made when it is used, since it cannot be stored for any length of time.

Weldwood glue	15 ozs.
Water	28 ozs.
Glycerine	14 ozs.
Wood Alcohol	6 ozs.

All measurements are by weight. If you like, you can substitute up to 5 ounces of ordinary wheat flour for the same amount of the glue. The solution should be thoroughly mixed before use, to make sure all the glue is dissolved.

A large tray can be made out of a sheet of Reynolds Do-It-Yourself aluminum. The corners can be cut out to allow bending up the four edges about 3 inches, then all the seams made liquid-tight with a bead of epoxy cement run into them. You might have to do two seams at a time and allow the cement to set before sealing the remaining corners. Burls and crotch veneers can be immersed in this solution for a couple of minutes, until well wetted, then stood on edge to drain thoroughly, until quite dry to the touch. After that the veneer is placed between metal sheets (two more sheets of the Reynolds aluminum will serve admirably), with a thick pad of newspaper on each side, and the metal sandwich placed between two plywood cauls with a light weight on top to dry.

The glue will serve to strengthen the veneer, and the glycerine will keep it flexible. The alcohol is added to evaporate the water which is necessary as a vehicle for the glue. Glycerine is highly hygroscopic and will take up a lot of moisture from the air, so the veneer should be allowed to dry for several days under the weights before running up into panels. Also, the gluing-up should be done on a dry day.

In extreme cases, where the veneer is still brittle after treatment, or where treatment would be undesirable because of danger of staining, it may be strengthened by gluing it up to a backing sheet. The veneer is first wetted thoroughly with hot water, then put between newspaper pads and boards under a weight to straighten them. After the veneer has become thoroughly dry it can be glued to the backing sheet. In the case of burls, perhaps the best material to use is heavy kraft paper, or thin muslin. When crotches are being worked, a sheet of straight grained mahogany or sapele would be better, with the grain of the backing sheet running the same way as the grain of the crotch veneer. This double sheet, then, can be worked as the face veneer, but allowance for the extra thickness of the backing sheet should be made when laying up the finished panel.

8

TAPING VENEERS

Taping the face and back veneers is a critical part of the entire operation of veneering. It is at this point that the quality of your panel is determined. Unless great care and patience is taken in taping, and the work checked carefully after the tape has dried and before the panel is laid up in the press, your entire work may be ruined and the material lost.

This is not to say that you must approach taping with fear and trembling. It does mean that you must take the time to work slowly, carefully, and accurately in all the operations.

With some veneers, especially the very hard ones such as ebony, rosewood, and snakewood, the face veneers can be taped with masking tape of the self-adhering type. It is not good practice to use this type of tape on soft woods. The enormous pressure will squeeze the adhesive right into the pores of the veneer and the tape will be stuck so firmly as to be nearly impossible to remove without pulling up the grain. Often the entire thickness of veneer may be pulled off the panel when pressure-sensitive tape is used. Masking tape is manufactured in several different conditions— maximum stretch, maximum adhesion, minimum stretch, minimum adhesion, and combinations of all four. If it is possible for you to find the different grades, the best one to use for taping up veneers is that tape with the minimum stretch and minimum adhesion. The maximum tapes are not as good because in the case of the stretch, they may allow the veneer to open at the taped joint, ruining the work. In the case of maximum adhesion, they might stick so tightly to the panel that the adhesive pulls off the tape and remains on the veneer when the tape is cleaned off the work. If this happens, the only way to remove the gum is to dissolve it with lacquer-thinner or benzine. The last is dangerous to use on light-colored woods because of the possibility of staining. Lacquer-thinner is better, even though it is more volatile and a bit more difficult to use.

Regular veneering tape is obtainable in veneer houses, hobby shops, and places which sell veneering tools. This is made of thin gummed paper, generally perforated along the length. Ordinary gummed paper sealing tape may also be used, and this comes in many different thicknesses and widths. About 1½-inch width is ideal for veneer work. Get the thinnest kind obtainable. It is much easier to get off the panel after removal from the press.

The tape must be held tightly against the wood and the two sheets being taped must be held rigidly in place with the matching marks exactly in position until the glue has dried on the tape. Otherwise there is a chance that the two sheets of veneer will slip apart before gluing the panel.

A few bricks covered with any kind of material, such as old carpet, canvas, thin leather, or even several thicknesses of muslin, are very handy tools for taping veneer and should be part of the equipment of every veneer shop.

With the face and back veneers all edged and the core stock prepared and crossbanded, you are ready to lay up the panel. On a flat surface large enough to contain the entire taped panel, lay out the veneer sheets in the order they are to be taped. Lay a covered brick on each end of the first sheet, leaving plenty of room at the joint for you to work with the tape. Slide the second sheet up against the first one and slip it up and down the length until the pattern is as close in match as you can get it. Lay a padded brick on the ends of the second sheet to hold it firmly in position.

The edge slippage should be not more than a fraction of an inch if the positioning of the veneers in the stack before you edged

81

them was accurately done. Actually, if all the matching and positioning were done properly from the very beginning of the operation, there should be no slippage necessary at all, but the sheets should fall into perfect alignment with all ends even, and the match accurate.

With the matched sheets held in position with the bricks or weights, fasten a short strip of masking tape across the joint at each end and in the middle pulling the stretch out of the tape before you press it in place. Working quickly before the tape stretches

The short holding strips are put on first, then the tape can be pulled between them.

enough to allow the joint to open, apply the gummed paper tape to the joint in lengths to fit between the masking tape holders. Do not put the gummed veneer tape over the masking tape, because you will then be unable to remove the masking tape before putting the panel into the press. A narrow flat board, wide enough to cover the tape, is placed on top of each strip of tape and held down with a heavy weight. Another brick will do nicely. Leave the weighted board in place until the gum on the tape has dried. Then you can remove the holding strips of masking tape and fill in with veneer tape which may now overlap the first strip if need be.

As a matter of fact, the short spaces where the masking tape was applied need not be covered with the veneer tape at all, unless the

82

veneer being used is curled or warped badly. If this were the condition of the veneer, then it should have been flattened before taping to begin with.

The next sheet of veneer is now brought into position, slid up and down until the match is made, then held in position with padded bricks as before, and the tape and weighted board put in place. Continue with this procedure until all the sheets are taped together, then allow at least two hours for all the tapes to dry.

The same method is employed to tape up the back veneer sheet. And it is good practice to tape up the back veneer first, allow the tapes to dry, then put it aside and tape the face veneers. This method is used to mimimize the possibility of breaking the face veneer while it is lying around the shop waiting for the back panel to dry. Since generally lower quality veneer is used for the back panels—the face veneer is the highly-figured one with the greatest amount of labor and cost in it—it is best to do everything possible to protect it until it is in the press.

Taping veneers which are not figure-matched, but which are put together in a pattern such as the panelled tabletop, shown on page 74, requires a different type of handling. When a panel is made up of two different veneers, the accent or dividing strip may be thicker or thinner than the body veneer. This is because the very rare and exotic veneers—ebony, rosewood, snakewood, and many other extremely hard woods often used for the accent strip—are not sliced to the standard $\frac{1}{28}$-inch thickness, but are, instead, sawn to $\frac{1}{20}$-inch thickness. The slight variation in thicknesses between the body veneers and the accent strips is enough to put the panel under unequal pressure right at the joint lines if this variation is not compensated for.

Perhaps the easiest way to compensate for the variation is to build up the thinner veneer with sheets of paper. A roll of heavy brown wrapping paper is a good addition to the veneer shop. Get a roll of the thickest paper you can find. One or at the most two sheets of this paper should make up the difference in thickness when you tape up and put the panel in glue. The pieces are first edged and taped. Then, before you start to glue the face and back veneers to the crossbanded core, you should pad the thinner spots with the paper. Carefully cut pieces of paper to the size and shape of the thin areas of veneer. The first sheet should not overlap the tape holding the veneers together, but should stop just short of it. A spot of glue or rubber cement in the middle of the paper sheet will hold it in position on the veneer, and this spot can easily be sanded off after the panel is removed from the press. Now cut a second sheet of paper to fill the entire thin veneer area, including lapping the paper tape holding the veneers together. This tape will act as one thickness of paper under the second sheet. If you lapped the tape with both sheets of filler paper, there would actually be three thicknesses of paper at the joint lines, reversing the trouble you are trying to overcome. The second sheet of paper can also be glued down to the first sheet, this time running a line of glue all around the edges to keep the sheet of paper from folding over when you are loading the panel into the veneer press. Since the face veneer side of the panel is placed down in the press, you may not notice if the paper filler sheets slipped or folded. Getting glue on the face veneer is nothing to worry about, since it will sand off when you finish the surface of the work, unless you are using a glue that stains and the veneer is a light color. In that case, use only rubber cement to fasten the filler paper in place, since this will not stain. After cutting all the paper filler sheets and gluing them in place, the panel of veneer may then be run through the normal gluing procedure. If for any reason you think there might be even a small possibility of the paper filler sheets buckling up when you load the press, then it would be wise to cover the entire panel, divide the strips and body veneers as well as the filler sheets with a large sheet of kraft paper, and glue it down all around the edges. The paper must cover the entire veneer assembly right out to the edges or it will impress a line in the veneer when under pressure. This covering sheet will hold all in place while you are slipping the panel into the press, and the additional thickness of the sheet of paper will be unimportant.

After the face and back sheets are taped you are ready to lay up the panel in glue. Place the back veneer on the gluing table with the clean side up—that is, the taped side down. Cut four or six lengths of masking tape about 4 inches long. Four lengths for panels up to about 4 feet long, six lengths for longer panels. Stick these lengths to the taped side of the back veneer, one in the center of each end, and one or two on each side. The tapes should be stuck about 1 inch onto the veneer, the remainder lying free with the sticky side up. Now position the core panel on top of the back veneer.

If the core stock is made out of commercial plywood, good one side, as is generally the case, the knot holes and defects should have been filled and sanded before the panel was crossbanded, and the side with the repairs marked so you know which is the good side. When the core is positioned on the back veneer as you have just done, the repaired side should be up and the good side down. Since the back is always put in glue before the front, the panel will fall into the correct position in relation to the sheets of face and back veneer.

The glue should be mixed according to the directions for the type you are using. It may be spread with a roller or a brush. The roller is faster and gives a more even coating. A paint roller core covered with a thin sheet of rubber or neoprene makes an excellent glue spreader. The cardboard core should be covered with glue and the rubber sheet wrapped around it tightly, being held in place with masking tape until the glue sets. If Weldwood glue is used, it will cure until it is practically waterproof, at any rate until the roller will withstand cleaning in hot water after each use.

Enough glue should be mixed to cover the entire surface of both sides in one thin even coating. It will take longer than the time you have to work to measure out the glue and water and mix them into a smooth liquid, and it is far better to throw away some glue than to run short with the panel only partly spread. I have found by experience that to cover both sides of enough panels to fill my 2-foot by 9-foot press, I must mix 20 ounces of dry glue with 12 to 15 ounces of water.

The glue is poured in a line down the center of the core panel,

The quickest way to spread the glue evenly is with a paint roller.

then spread evenly and *rapidly* over the entire surface. Care must be taken that there is not one single spot left uncoated, however small.

The coated panel is now lifted and reversed, then laid back on top of the back veneer sheet with the glue side down. Glue is now spread on the second side of the core panel and the face veneer sheet is laid on top of the glue with the taped side up.

The masking tapes that were stuck to the back veneer are now lifted up and pulled tightly around the edges of the sandwich to hold the back veneer to the face veneer while the entire assembly is put into the press. Work quickly, but without hysteria. You have

Pull the holding tapes tight around the edges as soon as you finish spreading the glue.

86

several minutes from the time you start to spread the glue until you close the press; while you are working the time seems to fly, but actually you have plenty of time if you do not dawdle. More than likely the first time you lay up a panel you will glue the veneer, yourself, any assistant you may have helping you together with the walls, floor, and ceiling of your shop. Keep right on going—you can wash up later. Right now the important thing is to *get the panel under pressure!*

Always slide the assembly into the press with the face veneer down. This gives the added distribution and weight of the core panel itself to the face veneer side. The panel should be set into the press resting at a low angle on the edge of one end, then slid into the press holding it up from the bed to avoid slipping the face veneer awry. When it is completely inside the press, drop your end

The "sandwich" should be slid in the press on one edge so the veneer will not be skidded out of position.

and immediately slide the top blanket plate in place. Keep the plate lifted up too, so you do not peel the veneer off the top of the assembly. Let the plate drop into place, and position it so it is exactly in line with the veneer press bed.

If the panel you are laying up does not fill the press, then the press must be filled with pads, or filler panels. These must be exactly the same thickness as the panel you are laying up. They do not have to be big panels, but can be small scrap pieces of cross-banded core stock with a scrap of face and back veneer stacked on

87

top. These filler pieces should be positioned at both ends and both sides if necessary. They will keep the press from bending the panel you are gluing when the pressure is applied. There will be a noticeable difference in thickness of the ends of a panel and its middle if filler pads are not used; the press will actually bow when it is tightened up and express the glue from the edges into the middle, humping up the face and back veneers.

With the filler pads in place, the two top blankets of the press are now slid in on top of the top blanket plate. The distribution bars are now positioned under the screws in each frame and the center screw of each frame is run down snug to close up the press. Now the press is run up tight and the panel is set to cure overnight.

As soon as the operation of closing the press is completed, wash out the mixing bowls and the spreading brush or roller with hot water. While the glue is still unset it will wash out easily, but if

When you slide this top metal blanket in place, be careful not to rip the veneer off the work with the front end of the metal.

you wait until the chemical reaction starts to take place you will never be able to get your tools clean. The glue may still seem green and loose, but it has started to cure and will not dissolve completely.

Not less than twelve hours should be allowed for the glue-line to cure. If you lay up the panel in the evening, it may be removed from the press the following morning. When you remove the panel from the press be extremely careful in handling it. There

Position the pressure bars squarely under each row of screws. Work as quickly as you can.

Always tighten the center row of screws first, then the edge rows.

will be many semicircular spills of hardened glue along the edges on the bottom side. These spills are razor-sharp and are dangerous. As mentioned earlier, you should have a pair of leather-palmed work gloves as protectors when removing panels from the press. The spills can be knocked off the edges before you work the panel, but always remember that they can cut you to the bone if you are not careful.

9

VENEERING CURVED PANELS

There are several ways to make curved panels. Perhaps the simplest way, if all the edges will be hidden either by being covered with veneer or by concealing joints, is by slitting. That is, the panel is made up in the veneer press just as though it were going to be a flat panel. Then, after all the veneering has been completed, the finished panel is slit on the back face with a thick blade on the table saw. Set the depth of cut to just leave the face veneer thickness remaining; the saw should cut through the entire thickness of the panel *except* the face veneer. Make repeated cuts across the panel, spacing them about ½ inch or ¾ inch apart. The sharper the bend the panel is to make, the closer the cuts should be.

After slitting the entire panel, brush the entire back face with glue, working it well down into the saw cuts. Wipe off the excess glue from the face of the panel, then bend it to the desired radius, slowly and carefully so as not to crack the face veneer. Hold the panel in the curved position by tacking a thin strip across the bow on both ends, and allow to stay until the glue has cured.

Now coat the back surface with contact adhesive, after sanding the surface smooth. Cut a sheet of crossbanding veneer to fit the curved panel; the grain of this sheet of crossbanding veneer should run across the saw cuts on the panel. This extra sheet of veneer will add strength and hold the panel in its curved position. Coat this with contact adhesive; contact adhesive will not make the panel warp as it would if you used a glue made up with water. When the adhesive is set, apply the crossbanding to the slitted back of the curved panel, working it well into contact with a roller or your hands.

Ideally, of course, a curved panel should be built up from scratch, out of multi-layered plywood. This operation is easier than it appears, but the thing to remember is that considerably more pressure is needed to make up a curved panel than to press a flat one. This is because there are several glue-lines to express instead of only two. The core will be made up of at least three plys, preferably five, and you will have crossbanding on both sides of the panel as well as the face and back veneers. If five plys were used, for instance, there would be eight glue-lines to express the glue from and to hold under pressure. This, theoretically, would require four times the pressure it takes to press up a regular panel with only two glue-lines to contend with. Actually, it takes a bit more, because, besides the extra glue-lines, there is the matter of the extra plys of wood which must be pressed flat and held so while the panel is in the press. Since no veneer is really absolutely flat when under glue, a certain amount of pressure is needed to hold it flat in the press.

Veneers of the total thickness of the panel you are making cannot be used, because, while the sum of the thicknesses of the veneers used in the core, crossbanding, and face and back veneers equal the desired thickness, you must also consider that there is a certain thickness on the glue-line. Especially when making a curved panel, your press is incapable of expressing the glue so completely that there will be no remaining thickness between the layers.

For example, if you are gluing up a flat panel $\frac{3}{4}$ inch thick, you would need five core veneers $\frac{1}{8}$ inch thick for the core, then two layers of standard $\frac{1}{28}$-inch crossbanding and the face and back veneers. This will total $\frac{3}{4}$ inch, not including the glue. However, the pressure is such on a flat panel that there is no work to be done to flatten the veneers, and all the energy is expended in expressing

91

the glue from between the layers. The panel will therefore turn out the desired ¾-inch thickness.

If you are curving a panel, much of the press energy is expended in bending the several layers of veneer, and the glue will not be entirely expressed from between the layers. The result is a thicker glue-line, and a resulting thicker panel.

If the work you are doing is made up entirely of the curved panel, this discrepancy in thickness does not matter, but if the curved panel is to be incorporated into a cabinet which also utilizes flat panels, then you must make an allowance for the thicker glue by reducing the thickness of the veneer core stock by a total of about $\frac{1}{16}$ inch. If you do this, then the curved panel will match the flat panels in thickness, even though the stock was scant, by virtue of having thicker layers of glue between each layer of veneer.

Poplar or mahogany are the best woods to use for this kind of core work. Poplar is readily available in these thicknesses, and in wide widths. Remember, of course, that the grain must run at right angles to the grain of the adjacent sheet at all times. Attention must be paid to the way you want the grain on the face veneer to run, and then adjust the grain direction of each successive layer down to the core. The back veneer must run the same way as the front veneer. In a 5-ply core, assuming that you want the face and back veneer grains to run the length of the panel, the core center sheet and the two outer core sheets would run the same way as the face and back veneers. The two inner core sheets (those right against the center sheet) and the two crossband sheets (directly under the face and back veneers) would run at right angles to the grain on the face and back veneers.

While you might be able to purchase poplar core veneer as wide as you want the panel to be, it is almost certain that you will be unable to get it as wide as the panel is long. Those layers which want the grain to run across the finished panel must be taped up to the desired width. If they were taped completely along their joints, the panel would have to be made up in stages. You would have to allow each taped layer to cure in the press, remove the partially complete panel to clean off the tape, then glue up the next layer. We must find a way to circumvent this.

If poplar or mahogany veneers are used for the core, they will probably be nice and flat, so you will not have to contend with the necessity of holding the veneers together when they are taped up to width. All you need do is hold the joints together until the assembly is put in glue, and this can be done with two or three shorts lengths of tape instead of taping the entire joint. Cut a few strips of tape into narrow widths—say, ½ inch or so, and about 2 or 3 inches long. Cut the veneers to the proper length and edge them for taping in the regular way. Pull the joints tightly together with short lengths of masking tape, then place a strip of the gummed tape across the joints about every foot and weight them until they dry. The masking tape may now be removed, leaving the veneers held by the regular veneer tape strips.

If these taped assemblies are handled carefully, they will hold together until the stack is made up and put under pressure. The narrow strips of tape will be glued right into the panel, but this should not cause any difficulty. They will be narrow enough not to pull loose after the glue-lines have cured, and short enough not to make a noticeable bulge in the face veneer. Taping the core stock this way we can put up the panel in one operation, which is certainly the easiest way to do the job.

Core veneer ⅛ inch thick may be stacked four high; one ⅟₁₆-inch-thick core veneer, then the crossbanding, and the face and back veneers. This will make a standard ¾-inch-thick panel to work with. The glue should be slightly thinner than usual. If Weldwood is used, instead of the usual 10-6 proportion, I would recommend 10 glue to 8 water. A slightly different sequence of gluing is followed. With all the veneers sized and taped in the special manner for curved panels, lay the back veneer tape side down on the gluing table and apply a coating of glue to its inner surface. Position a crossband veneer on top and apply a layer of glue to it, then follow with the outer core veneer, the inner core veneer, the center core veneer, the second inner core veneer, the second outer core veneer, the opposite crossband, and finally the face veneer, applying a glue coat between each layer. Tape together at the edges and run the assembly into the cauls and put into the press.

Caul construction is comparatively simple. The main idea is to get a contact surface over the entire area to be veneered. The caul must be rigid enough to force the veneer or the panel or both into the shape desired, instead of the caul bending out of shape itself when the pressure is applied. Not less than 2 inches of stock should be left at the lowest points in the caul, which would be, of course, the highest points on the panels.

A form must be made to the shape the finished panel is to take, and this form or caul must be in two parts—one to fit the convex side of the panel, and the other the concave side. In building the caul allowance must be made for the thickness of the finished panel, and the radii adjusted accordingly. The panel must be glued up to the finished thickness in the operation. About the easiest way to make a caul for a curved panel is to build it up out of a number of lengths of 2-inch-thick lumber, bolted together.

Bear in mind the need for the minimum amount of standing wood on the caul and select that width of lumber which, when the radius is cut out to make the form, will give it to you. Ordinary construction lumber comes in 4-, 6-, 8-, 10-, and 12-inch widths. Actually, these widths are slightly less, usually ⅜ inch narrower than the designated size. The length of the individual boards should be at least 4 inches more than the core of the panel you are making. The radius of the face is drawn on the side of a board and carefully bandsawed out. The piece that is removed should be saved and marked to correspond with the board it came from. Enough boards must be cut to cover the entire length of the panel under construction, with an inch of extra length at both ends.

When all the caul boards are cut to the correct radius, they are stacked accurately and drilled for bolting together. In the case of a long panel, they may be fastened together with lengths of threaded rod used as bolts. Not less than three and preferably five bolts

94

should be used to fasten the caul together; a coat of glue between each board will help stiffen the whole assembly. The bolts should be drawn up tight, then, after the glue has cured, tightened again. The inner surface of the caul should be lined with a pressure pad of Homasote or underlayment, and when laying out the radius for cutting, allowance should be made for the added thickness of the pad. The pieces taken out of each board may be used to make the caul for the back of the panel. This can be cut to fit inside the caul, allowing for the thickness of a pressure pad and the thickness of the panel being bent. This section of the caul, sometimes called the ram, is also glued and bolted together, and after assembling, a length of 2-inch-thick lumber is glued and screwed to the top edge of the ram to form a pressure area for the press screws to bear upon, and to stiffen the feather edges of the ram.

Never attempt to lay up a panel with a curve greater than a quarter circle; the strain of clamping and the height required for the caul makes this entirely impractical. In laying up panels for drum tables, for instance, each side of the table will be a bit less than a quarter circle, since the legs take up some space. For aprons or round or elliptical tables, the caul should be made to accomodate shorter sections. In the case of elliptical table aprons, a caul must be made to fit the different radii, and several cauls may be necessary to form up the entire ellipse. Bear in mind, of course, that each caul will form up a panel that will go in four positions on the table, right and left sides of each end. If your press is long enough to accomodate the caul, then the ellipse could be quartered and one caul do the entire job, provided the ellipse is not too elongated. If this were the case, the transition from the comparatively flat side to the sharp curve of the ends would be so abrupt that slippage would be very difficult if not impossible to eliminate when the work was placed under pressure. The tendency would be for the work to slide right out of the cauls. This difficulty might be eliminated by fastening a firm cleat at the flat end of the caul, against which all of the plys of veneer could be butted. The cleat should be enough higher than the end of the ram to form a support for the ram also, to keep it from skidding off the work along with the veneer.

Another method of making a core for a curved panel is to make it out of a number of narrow strips of lumber. While, actually, this will give you a curve generated as a series of narrow flats, still, if the radius is large enough, this method will serve and will save time and labor assembly.

The grain of these strips should run the same direction as the grain on the face and back veneers, since they will be bound together only with one layer of crossbanding which will have its grain at right angles to the face and back veneers. When cutting the strips for the core, they must be marked and alternated exactly the way you would do it if making up a flat lumber core. In the chapter on cores the method of alternating the grain of core lumber strips is explained. Follow the same idea when cutting these strips. However, the widest strip that should be used in making a core for a curved panel is about 1/2 inch. Since the strips are cut to 5/8-inch thickness, the standard thickness for the core of a 3/4-inch-thick panel, great care must be taken in assembling the panel and core to make certain that all the strips are right side up. The difference in the thickness and the width of such strips is so small that, in the bustle of assembly, gluing, and getting the whole into the cauls, it is very easy to tip one strip on its side, leaving a break in the uniformity of the panel, and, of course, ruining the panel. Since the error will not be noticed until the panel has cured and been removed from the press, it is well worth the extra and painstaking care to make sure everything is shipshape as you go along.

The greatest difficulty in making up a strip core, besides keeping all the strips in their position, is getting them brought into tight side contact with each other while the panel is under pressure. There is no convenient way of pulling up the layer of strips with a clamp which will hold them together while the crossbanding and face and back veneers are being pressed in place. Such 'a clamp would have to operate within the narrow 5/8-inch space of the core thickness, and it would have to pull the core together around a curve.

About the easiest way I have found to get around this problem is to saw a groove across both ends of each strip, from side to side. Incidently, this will serve as an additional guide toward keeping all the strips in their proper relation to each other when setting up the core. A length of stout wire is cut long enough to fit around the entire strip assembly with about 3 or 4 inches to spare.

Spread glue on the sides of all the strips and put them together in their proper position. Run the wire around the assembly, in the groove at each end and pull it up tight. Twist the ends together to put some pressure on the strips, but be careful that you do not twist the wire until it breaks, which is very easy to do. With the bound assembly in glue, now spread the glue on the back veneer and lay the first crossbanding sheet on top of the glue. Spread the crossbanding sheet with glue and lay the core on top of that. Spread the core with glue and lay the second crossbanding sheet in place. Then spread this with glue and lay the face veneer on the top of the stack, binding the whole together with short pieces of masking tape pulled around the edges. Carefully slide the assembly into the cauls and apply the pressure. As the pressure is applied the wire will tend to tighten up; it may even break. However, there should be enough pressure, by the time this happens, so that the core will not shift and pull apart.

Whenever you lay up a panel in a caul, it is good practice to make a dry run before putting all in glue. In a dry run, or dress rehearsal if you will, all the veneers, core stock, and crossbands should be stacked into the caul in exactly the way they will go in the final assembly, and the caul put in the press which is then tightened enough to bring all together as in the final operation. This will eliminate a lot of trouble in the assembly under glue, because you will be able to see the proper position to place the ram, the caul, judge the best sequence for tightening the press, etc. Perform this dry run just before you are ready to lay up the panel;

then proceed to the final stage while the dry run is still fresh in your mind.

Curved work may also be glued up and bent to shape in the same operation in cradles with a pressure surface of strips or tambours. The old fashioned roll-top desks were called tambour desks. The name tambour doors came from the same source. Tambours are strips of wood glued to canvas which are run in grooves to roll open or closed. In the case of veneering cradles, the tambours may be glued to canvas and kept as a flexible pressure plate, or they may be drilled on both ends and strung together on a thin nylon rope to allow for flexibility and conformation to the caul shape. The tambours should be at least 2 inches longer than the work.

The advantage of cradle work is the lightness of the form and the use of considerably less material to make it. For production of any number of panels or for hard curves, the caul is best, but for small doors or drawer fronts, a cradle is fine. To make this, three boards are needed for the base and three for the upper cradle or ram. The curvature of the desired panel is layed out in full size on a piece of smoothly sanded plywood or a large sheet of drawing paper. Draw the shape of the panel, exactly to size, and the ram and the cradle above and below the work. Allow space for the tambours, which should be not less than 3/4 inch thick.

After the drawing has been completed, the cradle patterns may be cut out of the plywood panel and the design transferred to 2 x 6 or wider lumber, depending on the amount of curvature you need in the cradle. You should use lumber wide enough to leave at least 2 inches of material standing at the lowest point in the curve. Three pieces are cut out of the lumber for the top and three for the bottom of the cradle, and these are now glued and screwed to a length of 2 x 10 lumber to make a base and a top support for the cradle members.

To glue up a panel in the cradle, the bottom tambours are laid in the cradle which is positioned in the veneering press. A thin sheet of aluminum is then laid on top of the tambours. The stacked panel in glue is layed on the metal plate and a second metal plate is placed on top, with the top tambours and lastly, the ram. The whole assembly is brought under pressure and allowed to stand until the glue has cured. Reynolds Do-It-Yourself aluminum sheets are excellent for this work. If the work is small, stainless steel Ferrotype tins as used in making glossy photographs are ideal tambour plates and will last for years. They are flexible enough to bend into the curves of the cradle, yet stiff enough not to allow the work to press in between the strips of tambours under high pressure. They come fairly large and are available in most large photographic supply stores. I have a pair of these plates that have seen service for over twelve years and are still as good as when they were first put into service.

Gentle curves, or work with a complicated compound curve may sometimes be set up in sand boxes or in rubber blocks. The method is applicable where the work is already curved, and merely wants to be veneered. It is not useful when you are bending the panel at the same time as veneering it. Serpentine drawers, if small enough and the curves gentle enough, can be veneered by this method to advantage, although for serpentine drawers the cradle or tambour clamp is best.

For sand-box veneering, the box must be very sturdy and very securely put together to withstand the tremendous side pressure when the press is run down. At least 4 inches of sand is necessary. More if practical, and if the sand is very slightly damp it is much better than if it were dry. The sand box is placed into the press and takes the place of the bottom caul or cradle. The work is coated with glue, then the face veneer is laid on the sand and the work laid on top of the face veneer. The work, backed up with a rigid board is laid on top and the press closed on the backing board. This method is useful only for small work and shallow curves. If the face veneer is of very hard or stiff wood, it might help to make an impression by forcing the work into the sand first to make the cavity, then proceeding as before.

Rubber-pressing is much the same thing as sand. Here, however, a block of rubber is used in place of sand. The box holding the rubber should be strong and securely made to withstand the pressure. The rubber should be about 2 inches thick. It is available in sheets of different densities, and is used in shallow drawing of metals in much the same fashion as veneering. This method of pressing is useful with some of the more rigid veneers if applied to gently curved surfaces. Exactly the same method as that used in sand pressure is employed. The face veneer is laid on the rubber and the core and back veneer laid on top of it. The ram is placed on top and the whole then run up tightly in the press. Sand box and rubber block veneering finds its best use, in fact, its only use, in applying the face and back veneers or the crossbanding, to work which has been pre-curved. When serpentine drawers are being made, usually the drawer fronts are bandsawed out of thick lumber to the curve desired. This wavy piece of wood, generally cut out of good grade mahogany, is then face and back veneered. This application is ideally performed in the sand box, and, in the case of small work, in the rubber block press.

One problem you might have with sand box veneering that you will not encounter in the rubber mold, is that of sand sticking to the edges of the panel. This might not seem too great a difficulty, and indeed it is not, if you are aware of it. However, if you take such a panel out of the sand box and attempt to joint one edge true to size up the panel, you will very likely have to invest in a new set of jointer blades, since the grains of sand are extremely hard and will badly damage the edges of woodworking tools.

It is a simple enough matter to scrape the edges clean of sand grains with a small hook scraper before putting the work on to any power machine such as a saw or jointer. When scraping an edge— and I might take this opportunity to mention that scraping a sandy edge is the only time a hook scraper should be used on veneers with one exception—always scrape towards the center of the core with the scraper held askew to the edge of the panel. This will give a slight shearing action to the scraper and minimize the possibility of ripping the veneer off the faces of the panel. The one exception mentioned above is when you are scraping the tape off a finished panel. The paper itself can be removed easily with a hook scraper, but you should not attempt to clean the surface glue off the veneer with anything but a sander. The danger of pulling holes into the surface of the face veneer is too great to warrant the use of a hook scraper. Cabinet scrapers can be used to cut the saw marks off the surfaces of panels veneered in very hard woods such as ebony, rosewood, snakewood, and similar species. This will save much sanding time and also tend to give a smoother surface.

On occasion you may want to veneer a curved panel which has already been made up into a piece of furniture. Perhaps it is in the nature of a repair, the original veneer having peeled or become damaged in some way. Or it is possible that you have a manufactured piece you would like to improve with a better grade of veneer over the old surface. In any event, this type of work can be done by using contact adhesive instead of glue, and by using an inflatable bag for your pressure pad.

Surplus stores and scientific equipment places offer for sale large government surplus balloons at a very low cost. Some of these are so large as to be useless, but I have several that inflate to 3 feet and 5 feet. These are made of very thick rubber and are very strong. When veneering already assembled work on curved surfaces, it is a simple matter to apply pressure with one of these balloons. Partially inflate the balloon until it holds its shape, then prepare the work for gluing. Apply the contact adhesive according to the directions on the can. Generally this means two coats should be applied to both the veneer and the work, and the adhesive allowed to dry between coats and after the last coat as well. After applying the veneer to the work, the balloon is used to bring pressure to bear on the curved panel in this way: back the balloon against a wall of your shop and ram the cabinet up against the balloon so as to wedge it in place securely. A couple of long planks slid between the cabinet and the opposite wall would be ideal. Now inflate the balloon as much as you can, using a bicycle or automobile tire pump if you do not have a compressor. Be careful not to explode the balloon, though if it is one of the really tough ones, that will take a lot of doing. The balloon will take the shape of the work very completely and apply an even pressure to the panel. With contact adhesive, you need only put the pressure on for a few minutes, then the affair can be released by letting the air out of the balloon. A light tapping all over with a rubber-faced mallet will help insure good contact.

For veneering round surfaces, such as a cylinder for a lamp, pressure can be applied by wrapping the object while it is in glue. Very thin veneer is best to use for this work. Some kinds of woods are available in veneers $\frac{1}{50}$ and $\frac{1}{100}$ inch thick; some are also cloth backed. If the particular veneer you want to use does not come in thin or cloth-backed condition, then, of course, you will have to use the standard thickness of $\frac{1}{28}$ inch. With most veneers this will not present an insurmountable problem, however, since you can flexibilize the veneer before using it as an aid in bending it around short radii. The same solution used to treat burls (p. 78) could be used, or as an alternative, the veneer could be wetted with a solution of glycerine and water, in the proportion of 8 ounces of glycerine to 1 gallon of water. In recent times I have tried a different solution to work veneers, and this seems to be very good for this purpose. This is a photographic flattening solution made for the purpose of keeping photographs, particularly glossy prints, from curling after they have been dried. The solution is mixed according to the directions on the bottle, and I should recommend the "very dry day" mixture as printed in the mixing directions. If the veneeer is soaked in this solution for about ten minutes, then put to dry under light pressure for several days, changing the pads of newspaper daily, the same way as for flattening warped veneers, you should find it quite flexible and easy to bend around the form.

With relatively soft wood veneers of more or less straight grain, you may be able to make the bend with no treatment at all except care not to make the bends too sharp. If the piece you are working on is not a simple round cylinder, you should not try to make dry bends, but treat the veneer before putting it around the base.

Treating the veneer with steam from a teakettle spout will soften it enough to allow you to make quite short bends. The veneer should be steamed immediately before you apply it to the base. The trouble with steaming is that, if you get the veneer very damp, it may shrink in drying on the base causing the joint to pull open or cracks to appear around the work.

About the biggest difficulty you will encounter in gluing veneer to a cylinder is in getting a perfectly flat, tight joint. Bear in mind that the joint in the veneered cylinder is exactly the same as a joint in matched veneer for a panel; the same care must be taken to produce a closed, tight seam. Multiplying the diameter by Pi or wrapping a paper or string around the cylinder to get the measurement for the veneer are not accurate enough. There are several ways to get the accurate length of veneer to wrap a cylinder. Select the sheet of veneer you want to use and true up one edge on your edger board. With a very sharp pencil, draw a line from one end to the other of the cylinder, then position the trued edge of the veneer exactly on the line, holding it in place with a couple of small tacks driven through the veneer into the cylinder as close to the edge of the veneer as you can without splitting the veneer. Wrap the sheet *tightly* around the cylinder, overlapping the edge that you fastened down. Then mark the top and bottom with a sharp pencil exactly on the overlap. The veneer sheet may now be removed from the cylinder and positioned very carefully in the edger exactly on the marks and the second edge trued up.

Another method, one that allows more leeway for error, may be a bit easier. Drive a very thin brad into the cylinder at the top and bottom, exactly on a line drawn down the length of it. Allow not more than the tiny head of the brad to stick out. Now file the heads on both sides to form them into a very sharp chisel point. Make certain that you file evenly on both sides so the "cutting" edge of the chisel is directly on the pencil line drawn on the cylinder. The accuracy with which you file the heads determines the accuracy of the finished joint, so take your time.

Now, place the sheet of veneer you want to use on a flat surface and lay the cylinder on it. Roll the cylinder until the sharpened

103

brads are at the bottom, and near one edge of the veneer. Gently press the cylinder on the veneer until the chisel heads of the brads stick into the veneer and make a mark. Without lifting the cylinder, and taking great care that it does not slip in any direction, start to roll it across the sheet of veneer. Be careful to make sure that the brads lift out of the veneer when you start the rolling, and that they do not pick the veneer up and carry it around the cylinder. Roll the cylinder until the brads again come into contact with the veneer and again press them into the veneer to make another pair of marks. The veneer may now be trimmed near the marks to remove most of the excess material, and the sheet then carefully positioned in the edger and edged exactly to the two sets of marks.

Still another way, and this is a variation of the previous one, is to true one edge of the veneer first, then, when filing the brad heads, file them to a sharp chisel point, but on one side only. The other side is filed vertically flat, with the edge of the flat exactly on the pencil line on the cylinder. The side away from the flat is filed to the chisel point. With the veneer on the flat surface, lay the cylinder on the veneer with the brads off the finished edge, and slide it up until the flat sides of the brads are tight against the finished edge of the veneer. Now roll the cylinder across the veneer as before until the brads stick into it after a complete revolution, and the sheet may then be edged to the single pair of brad marks.

Whatever method you use to determine the exact size of the veneer, your difficulty will be to get the joint to lie flat. It is hard to clamp a cylinder with equal pressure, evenly applied, all over the surface. Veneer will always tend to straighten itself out, even if it has been flexibilized, and the place where the straightening will take place is the quarter-inch or so on each side of the seam.

If you are using mixed glue, about the easiest way to clamp the veneer is to wrap the cylinder like a mummy with automobile friction tape. This tape will stick to itself and let you draw it very tight, but will not stick to the veneer. Wind a slow spiral tightly around the cylinder, layer on layer for at least three layers, pulling the tape to the limit of its strength, especially on the first wrapping. Be sure to place the veneer on the cylinder with one edge exactly on the line to start. Use glue that is a bit thinner than ordinary, and coat the cylinder as sparingly as you possibly can and still cover the entire surface. The excess glue has no place to go when you clamp up, as is the case with flat work in the press where the excess can squeeze out the two sides of the panel. Theoretically the excess glue could squeeze out both ends of the cylinder, too, but this can happen only when pressure is sufficient to expel the glue. In this case, enough pressure would be difficult if not impossible to obtain. A cylinder can also be glued up with contact adhesive, if you are able to pound the seam flat and tight. It might be a good idea to lay a narrow strip of wood along the seam after applying the veneer, and bind all tightly together for an hour or so to insure good contact at the joint. Rolling the cylinder on the table as though you were rolling dough will help make the joint tight, and help to bring the entire surface of the veneer into good contact as well.

If you are making a lamp, always veneer the sides of the cylinder *before* you veneer the flat (top and bottom) ends. This will allow the flat veneer to lap over the thin edges of the side veneer and reduce the chance of chipping or pulling at the side seam when the lamp is handled. In general, any veneered piece should have the top surface veneered after the sides, for the same reason—protection of the edges.

10

EDGING VENEERED PANELS

After the panel has been cut to size, it is ready for edging. The edges of veneered panels are finished according to the use the panel is to be put to. If it is the top of a chest, for instance, the edges should be square, and they should be veneered with strips cut from a sheet of the same veneer used for the surface.

In edge-veneering, you can proceed in either of two ways. You can use the same kind of glue as was used to lay up the panel, i.e., resin glue, in which case clamps and clamping cauls must be employed, and the two opposite edges glued simultaneously; or you may use the contact adhesive cement, with which you may work all around the panel one edge after another. For panels that are protected from knocking and abuse, contact cement is ideal.

For gluing edge-veneers the edge of the panel must be jointed smooth and square. Do not sand after jointing, to avoid rounding the edges of the face and back veneers which must be sharp and square in order to show no mark at the glue-line. Also if the edges of the face and back veneers are rounded, the edge veneer may be caught and pulled off the panel while finishing, or when in use.

Following the first method, make a caul not less than 2 inches thick and 1 inch wide, and cover the gluing face of the caul with a strip of wallboard or underlayment. Homasote makes a good gluing pad for this purpose. Fasten the pad to the caul with some quick-setting glue such as Elmer's or any other adhesive. Do not use contact cement for this purpose, because under the steady pressure over an extended period of time, the pad might slip off the caul and the caul loosen in the clamps. A good way to glue the pads to the cauls is to prepare a pair of cauls and pads, then apply the glue to one face of each caul, lay the pads on, then lay a strip of waxed paper along the pad and put the second pad and caul on the waxed paper. The whole may then be clamped up with hand-screws or C-clamps, and the cauls will themselves act as clamping bars to hold the pads in position while the glue is setting.

A roll of waxed paper, cut into widths to fit the edge cauls will protect the pad surfaces and allow you to use the cauls for years without having to replace the pads. When gluing the edge of a panel, a strip of the waxed paper is taped to the surface of the pad with a piece of masking tape at each end. With the panel across two horses, adjust three bar clamps to span the panel with the cauls in place at opposite sides. Then apply glue to the opposite edges, lay the strip of veneer in place and hold it there with three strips of masking tape brought around the edge of the panel and stuck to the face and the back surfaces. Position the cauls, covered with waxed paper so there is an equal overlap on both sides of the panel, and clamp all together with one clamp in the middle of the panel. Turn the assembly over on the horses, place the other two clamps on each side of the panel, and pull all tight. Alternating the clamps this way keeps the panel flat while the glue is setting.

After the glue has hardened, remove the clamps and cauls, strip the waxed paper from the cauls and replace it with a fresh strip. With heavy shears or a very sharp knife, cut the excess veneer off close to the work at both ends of the strip. Using a wide smooth file, or one of the flat tungsten-carbide files now available in al-most every hardware store, file the veneer flush with the raw edges of the panel. Work from the veneered edge toward the panel, to avoid pulling the freshly glued veneer off the edge. When you have finished the first two edges, repeat the process for the two remaining edges, overlapping the first two veneers at the corners. The usual system for edge veneering a table top, for instance, is to veneer the front and back edges first, then the ends. In this way

107

the end veneers overlap the front and back veneers and there is less chance of pulling off the edges.

If you ever have to veneer an edge which is shaped in multiple curves, reverse curves, or cove corners, where the edges of the coves or curves terminate in an actual corner, then the inside or concave part of the curve is always veneered *before* the rest of the edge. It is far easier to finish down the overlap from the edge veneer to a flat surface, than it is to try to finish into a curve. In cove corners especially, this is very difficult, and the cove should be veneered first. Care must be taken when veneering a concavity to hold the veneer strip away from the work while you are applying it. Since the strip of wood will try to straighten out all the time, there is a good possibility of its touching some part of the edge and adhering tightly. This would be considerably difficult to remove and might even necessitate re-working the entire edge. Contact adhesive, when properly applied sticks tenaciously even if the glued strip barely touches the work. Fortunately the narrow strips of veneer used for the edges are flexible enough to allow you to bend them away back without snapping them.

You may often want to veneer the edge of a panel, as for instance a large table top, which has been thickened by the addition of boards along the edges to make the panel appear as though it were made out of 2- or even 3-inch.lumber rather than 3/4 inch. At times, these thick edges are veneered with the grain running the long way, but they look very much richer if you veneer them with the grain running the short way. This is called vertical-grain edging, and it has several advantages in edge-finishing. First, it is possible to use up a lot of short cuttings of veneers that way. Then, too, you will be working with many short lengths instead of long strips. With contact adhesive, this is a decided advantage, because you will not have to be watching all the time you are working to make sure you are not letting the strip fall onto the edge where it is not supposed to touch. Also, with long strips you must start it in contact exactly true, or part way down the panel you will find the strip running off the panel edge. When this happens, there is absolutely nothing you can do about it, but plane or sand it off and start all over again.

In vertical-grain edging, the match of grain from piece to piece is not so important as long as the general grain, color, and texture of the adjacent pieces are close. Naturally, the optimum would be to match up each piece as carefully as you would the face veneers on the panel, but this is not really necessary on the edge.

Most thick table tops have the corners rounded, and the veneer must be carried right on around the curve. In softwood veneers such as sapele, mahogany, and avodire, this does not present too much of a problem, since the veneer is flexible enough to bend sideways in a small radius. With rosewood, ebony, and other hard veneers, however, you would be in trouble trying to force them into the bend. The easiest way to overcome this problem is to either turn a cylinder on the lathe to the exact radius, or a bit smaller than that of the corners, and use this for a molding form; or, if you do not have a lathe or access to one, a glass jar can almost surely be found with a diameter close enough to the corner curve you are working with. Actually, anything cylindrical in form of the proper size will do except a cardboard tube. This cannot be used because it would fall out of shape when it became wet and was put under pressure.

With a form handy, a piece of veneer long enough to carry around the corner—or if the span is too great, two or more pieces—is squared up and both edges trued on the edger board. These are then placed in a saucepan of water, the water is brought to a boil and let simmer for a few minutes. Then remove the pieces one at a time from the boiling water and lay them on the cylinder. Be careful to put them on squarely so the curve will be at right angles to the matching edges of the veneer pieces. Wrap them with several turns of friction tape, working quickly to get the veneer taped down tightly before it cools. If the form is long enough you may be able to put more than one piece of veneer on it at the same time. Otherwise, only boil enough to fill the form at one time.

Leave the taped veneer on the form for a day or so. If the form is a glass jar, the veneer should remain taped to it for at least two days, since the evaporation of the water will take place very slowly. If the form is of wood, the veneer should dry very well within a day. It might be an excellent idea to oven-dry the veneer by putting it in the oven at the lowest temperature setting, especially if you are using a glass jar for the form, and let it bake for not less than three or four hours to evaporate all the water.

On removal from the form the veneer will have taken a set and, while it may spring back somewhat, it can be easily fitted to the corner. As a matter of fact, you will have to spring it open a bit as you put it in place, since it is almost impossible for you to slap a curved piece of veneer onto a curved corner exactly in the proper position.

When applying the contact adhesive to the edge veneers, be very careful not to get the adhesive on the matching edges. There is an actual body to the contact adhesive that will tend to hold the two adjacent pieces of veneer apart, allowing the joint to show. Nothing is more unsightly than an open or sloppy glue line in veneering.

Sometimes tables, especially low coffee tables, are made with an apron and a drawer or two. When you are making this kind of piece, the veneer for the edges and for the apron should be matched, and the drawers cut out of the matched apron; then when the drawers are closed the pattern of the veneer will be continuous. Almost always the veneer on the apron will be vertical grain, and the edges will be the same. The veneers selected for the apron should be cut long enough to allow for the edge veneers from the same piece. The part assigned to the edges should be sliced off the matched apron veneers and marked so you will be able to put it on the edges of the panel directly above the part it was taken from, which will be on the apron below. The extra time and trouble it takes to fit the two sections together as to pattern continuity is well paid for in the appearance of the finished work.

Often the edge of a panel is bevelled instead of square. When this is the case you should never bevel the edge to a knife edge, but always try to leave at least ⅛-inch flat. A knife edge is very unstable and subject to easy damage; the small flat will help prevent this. Since the bevel is almost invariably on the bottom of the edge instead of on the top, such an edge is rarely veneered with vertical grain. The best way to finish this kind of edge is to size the panel and finish the edges for veneering all around just the way you would do if you were making a square edge. After the four edges have been veneered, they may be bevelled and the remaining edge will have the veneer already on it. The bevel may now be veneered. This leaves the joint of the two intersecting edge veneers very sharp, but, since the edge is so drawn out, there is quite a bit more veneer at the joint than normally. You will therefore be able to sand a very small radius to merely break the sharpness of the edge without sanding through the veneer. Just two or three passes with fine paper is all you have to do .

The edges of a panel are always veneered before the panel is fitted to the article of furniture. All preliminary sanding is done before assembly, as well, but be careful not to round off any edges or ends that are going to be part of a joint. The edges of veneers must be kept sharp and square at each joint, or you will have an unsightly line after the work is assembled.

If your panel is going to have a central panel of fancy veneer and a frame or border around it—with or without an inlay strip— then the edges should be veneered first. After all edges are veneered and the preliminary sanding done, cut the rabbet for the border frame routing down the veneer to the panel edge at the same time. Then, when the border is glued to the panel, it will lap the edge veneer and the joint will be tight and invisible. There will be enough material in the lap to allow the light sanding needed to break the edges without sanding through the veneer.

Fancy shaped edges are not practical to veneer. Such shapes as ogee, thumbmold, and tablemold are best done in lumber edges which may be made up in the panel while finishing it, or glued to the core stock before veneering it.

111

Many times doors for cabinets are made with each door being one half of the veneer pattern. When the doors are closed, the opening between them becomes the match-line of the veneers. Such doors are generally framed with a contrasting veneer border, and often this border is carried around both doors so that it, too, matches up when the doors are closed to form a continuous border around both panels.

Generally the same veneer is used on the edges of such doors as was used on the frame, except for the inner edges. These can be given a different treatment. If the doors are left ajar, as is often the case, the inner edge of the open door is visible. If the edge was veneered with the frame veneer, the edge stands out as a broad band right down the middle of the door. Of course, one way to eliminate this unsightliness is merely to close the door. Here is another solution to the problem: veneer the inner edges of matched and mating doors with the border or frame veneer, the inlay strip, or the central panel veneer made up to exactly match that on the face of the panel. In this way, even if the door is left ajar, the pattern and color of the two doors is uninterrupted.

11

INLAYS AND BORDER STRIPS

Often a piece of furniture may be enhanced by the addition an of inlay border or inlay design set into the face veneer. It is much easier to do the inlaying after the panel has been glued up and finished, rather than to attempt to tape the inlay into the sheet of veneer before pressing.

The border strip is best used, not to make a fancy edging around a panel, necessarily, but to set off a frame or to act as a divider between the main panel—if a burl, for instance—and the edge wood, which would be a plainer figure. The best use of burls is as a center panel, using a very plain veneer for the frame, with an unobtrusive border strip separating the frame from the panel. Well-made borders beautify the finished work considerably, when used with taste and judgment. They can also cheapen a piece of otherwise fine furniture if used indiscriminately, or when a border is mismatched to the face veneer.

Inlay designs can be used as a focal point when diamond-matching a center panel, as accent points on wide table legs, or as an expedient to eliminate what would otherwise be a difficult joint to match. For instance, if a table top were being veneered in a wedge pattern, with four, six, eight, or more segments tapering to a point in the middle, the veneer would have to meet in a hair-line point and the joint would be most difficult to make, if not indeed impossible. Here a center inlay design, selected to blend with the total scheme of the panel, would save hours of tedious work and make possible a fine panel. The inlay design would eliminate the necessity of shaving the veneers to sharp points; the joints would meet at the edges of the design instead.

To inlay a design, the veneers are matched up and the panel put in the press in the usual manner. After cleaning up and trimming, the design is set into the surface of the panel and the panel returned to the press, or, if it is small enough, the design can be clamped under glue with a large handscrew or heavy weight.

The design is set in place in the exact position it is to occupy, and with an extremely sharp hard pencil the outline traced carefully to the face veneer. The cavity to receive the pattern is then cut out with chisels or an electric router with a flat cutter set to the thickness of the face veneer. Generally the inlay designs are made out of veneers slightly thicker than the ordinary veneer. This is to allow easier clamping when gluing into a panel, and to allow extra stock for sanding flush with the panel surface.

When using a router to cut out the cavity, extreme care must be used not to cut out over the line. It is best, if possible, to outline the shape and size of the cavity with a small very sharp chisel and chisel out a narrow border just within the outline. The remainder of the wood may then be easily removed with the router without danger of going beyond the outline. It is also good practice to cut the cavity a few thousandths of an inch smaller than the pencilled mark, since no matter how sharp the point of the pencil you are bound to have a slight extra thickness of line that would make the inlay design loose in the cavity. If you leave the entire pencil line standing when you cut the cavity out, you should be safe. The design can be lightly sanded around the edge to allow it to be pushed snugly into place. To secure the inlay design, use a very thin coating of glue, bearing in mind that excess glue has no place to go when pressure is applied, and if you apply too much glue the inlay design might buckle and crack under the hydraulic pressure of the glue.

Inlay designs are supplied to the craftsman glued to a sheet of paper, and with scrap veneer all around the edges to protect the inlay. This scrap veneer must be removed before inlaying, but the paper must be left attached. The paper holds the number of tiny pieces of veneer used to make up the design all in place until the whole is glued into a panel. The inlays are set into the panel with the paper side up, and, after the glue has cured, the paper and excess thickness of the inlay are sanded down flush with the face of the panel.

A great number of designs are available in inlays, some of them very complicated. The simpler, geometric designs are in the best taste when used as a centerpiece for a panel. The designs are really a form of marquetry, made up of a number of small pieces of different kinds or different colors of veneers. When the design is colored, they are usually made of some soft wood, such as poplar or whitewood, and dyed.

Sometimes parts of the design will be made of veneers that are shaded from pale to dark brown. This shading effect is obtained by scorching. A flat tray of sand is heated, and the veneers are stuck into the sand edgeways. The pieces are stuck in only part way. Continue to heat the sand leaving the veneer pieces in until they begin to scorch. The amount of scorching determines the depth of tone on the veneer, and the distance the piece is stuck into the sand determines the area of coloring. Shading can be done very cleverly, and the resultant inlay is very good looking. This method of coloring lends itself well to sunburst designs and similar patterns, where the only contrast between the individual pieces of veneer used to make up the inlay is the shading at one edge of each piece.

When setting up a shading tray, it should be placed on a burner-type of heater—not in an oven. This is because the air around the protruding veneer should be relatively cool, and the only heat applied to the veneer should come from the sand. If you put the shading tray in an oven, there would be a good possibility of scorching the entire piece of veneer, and, while you might get a good shade of tan or brown, it would be an all-over color, not a shading. The finer the sand used in the tray, the more even the shading will be on the veneer. If it is scorched too much, the veneer will be useless as in inlay, since it will char through and crumble. Just enough scorching should be given to turn it dark at the bottom of the edge. Remember that you are going to sand the finished inlay after it has been glued in place. The sanding will take off quite a bit of the dark color, so scorch the pieces several shades darker than you want the finished color to be. A few trial pieces will tell you about how dark the scorching should be.

Dye-shading might also be done for certain effects, by using a strong dye solution and suspending the pieces of veneer in such a manner that one edge just touches the surface of the dye. The color will be absorbed into the wood by capillarity and will be the darkest at the point of contact with the dye solution, shading to lighter as the dye is sucked up into the wood. Color-fast fabric dyes might be used, and these are obtainable in large grocery stores and supermarkets. Make them up with about one-quarter of the water normally used, even stronger if you want deep colors. Here, again, the pieces should be dyed a bit darker than the desired finished color, to allow for the lightening effect of sanding.

One hundred years and more ago, the Dutch were fond of making ornately curved chests of drawers, covered with inlays of veneers. Shading was much employed, but the most intricate pieces were made of hundreds and even thousands of small pieces of veneers fitted together so precisely that the joints were almost invisible. The design was of great intricacy—bouquets of flowers, birds, and animals being the most common. The effect was achieved by the painstaking selection of veneers having the color as a natural part of the wood, rather than by using dyes or shading. The overall effect, while ornate and complicated, was still very pleasing, being an example of the fact that "noble" woods do not clash when used together.

Very intricate inlay border strips are available in houses that sell tools and accessories for veneering. Albert Constantine and Sons, Bronx, New York, and H. L. Wild, New York City, both carry an excellent stock of inlay border strips and inlay designs. These come in 3-foot-long pieces and are very reasonably priced, considering the amount of work it takes to make them.

Dozens of patterns are regularly carried in stock, but while the overall pattern is the same, each piece made up will vary slightly in the size and placement of its components. A length from one lot may not exactly match a length from another lot. It is always good practice, therefore, to buy a length or two more than necessary to make sure the pattern is exactly the same if you need a replacement or extra piece for any reason. For the same reason, always get the full amount needed for each new job—even if you have a length or two left over from another job. Do not try to fill in with what you have on hand.

The manufacture of these inlay strips is interesting, and should be described here. Because often there is a need for an inlay border strip that is not made commercially, or not available when it is wanted, the veneersman should know how to put them together. It is a good idea to start with simple ones, and ones that can be made out of stock thicknesses of veneer. One of the most used strips is made of holly (or poplar), ebony (or black dyed veneer), and tulipwood. The center is made of a thick sheet of tulipwood, anything from $\frac{3}{32}$ to $\frac{3}{16}$ inch thick. A piece about 8 or 10 inches wide and 36 inches long is needed for one slab of inlay. If the tulipwood is narrower than 8 or 10 inches, it can be edged and glued together just as though you were matching it for veneering, only you need not pay any attention to the actual matching of the grain. A piece of ebony or dyed wood of standard $\frac{1}{28}$-inch thickness is placed on top and on the bottom of the tulipwood, and a piece of the same thickness holly or poplar is placed on top of the ebony. You now have a sandwich composed of whitewood, blackwood, tulipwood center, blackwood, and whitewood again. Spread the tulipwood on both sides with a thin coating of glue, put the next sheets in place and spread them with glue, adding the top and back sheets and slide the whole into the veneer press. Since this is a small area, really, it can be pressed up between two thick boards with a pad of Homasote between, and ringed around with hand-

117

screws for pressure. Allow to cure overnight, then true up one edge on the jointer, and slice it on the table saw with a very thin, fine-toothed blade, preferably a hollow-ground veneer blade. The slices should be about $\frac{1}{20}$ inch thick; this can be gauged by comparing a slice with a piece of veneer of that thickness. Slice after slice is made until the entire sheet is cut, and the strips put in stock against the time you want to use them.

Variations can be made. For instance, with the same tulipwood center, you can place the blackwood in the outside and the whitewood on the inside next to the center. Generally, the last layer is selected to contrast with the veneer on the panel to which the inlay border strip will be applied. If the panel veneer is a dark wood, then the whitewood layer should be on the outside. If the panel veneer is one of the light, pale woods such as avodire, limba, or satinwood, then the black layer is the outside layer to make a better contrast. A popular strip made up of these three woods is available in the supply houses. The difference—and this is useful in many places where the grain of the border makes an important addition to the overall appearance of the panel—is that the grain of the tulipwood center is vertical (across the narrow width of the strip) instead of long-grain.

Making up inlay border strips is an excellent spare-time hobby, and it is always handy to have a supply of them in stock. There is really no limit to the designs possible. These depend only upon your ingenuity and patience, and the availability of the veneers for the component parts. In general, the harder woods are the best for inlay strips, but teak, cocobola, and a few other very oily woods are not practical. Because of the great amount of oil in the woods, the glue may not hold securely, especially after it has been cut into thin strips, and there is a good danger of the strip falling apart after it has been sliced.

In making up the sandwich for strips having a pattern of blocks or designs along the length, the central section is built up first out of the component pieces. Since the individual strips are sliced off the length of the sandwich or stack, bear in mind that the grains of the parts of the design should be side grains, not end grains. This is to say, if you use long individual strips to serve as the different components of a block inlay strip, then, when it is sliced after gluing up the stack, all the block parts of the design would be end grain. This is not what you want.

Let's see what we need to build up the center core of an inlay strip made of alternate blocks of rosewood and satinwood, with spacers of ebony, and the outer layers also of ebony. First, the blocks of rosewood and satinwood can be cut. You will need $\frac{5}{32}$ material, either 10 inches wide or narrower pieces glued up to make that width, of both rosewood and satinwood. The thing you must be sure of is that both the woods are the same thickness. Square up one end of each piece of wood, then slice off strips $\frac{3}{8}$ inch long across the width. This will give you pieces 10 inches wide and $\frac{3}{8}$ inch long, with the grain running the short distance in the piece. Very short pieces of wood are very fragile; handle them carefully, or they will snap into little pieces which will make them more difficult to manage when assembling the sandwich.

With the rosewood and the satinwood cut to size, you will need a number of spacer strips of ebony veneer. The standard $\frac{1}{20}$-inch veneer is fine, and strips 10 inches long and exactly as wide as the rosewood and satinwood is thick should be cut. The grain can run the long way on these, since they will be used only as color spacers, and they will be so thin that there will be no grain showing. You now need two sheets of ebony veneer 10 inches wide and 36 inches long for the top and bottom. You are ready to glue up the core, but before doing so, we have to figure out a way to hold them together.

The easiest way is to cut two sheets of metal—either the do-it-yourself aluminum sheeting that hardware stores sell, or sheet zinc from the local sheet-metal worker. They should be 11 inches wide and 36 inches long. Four sheets of $\frac{3}{4}$-inch plywood are needed. Each pair of these is glued together to make one sheet $1\frac{1}{2}$ inches thick, by 10 or 11 inches wide and 36 inches long. These are the gluing blankets and stripper sheets. Next you need two bars of

119

steel, ⅛ inch thick by 1½ inches wide and 11 inches long. These are the pressure cauls.

We are *now* ready to assemble. You will need approximately 54 strips each of the rosewood and satinwood, and about 108 of the ebony strips. Cut several extra of each in case any snap while you are assembling.

Lay one plywood clamping board on the bench and one sheet of metal on top of it. Then, with the stock at hand, start to glue up by putting a layer of glue on one side of a rosewood strip and laying it on the metal plate about an inch from one side. Glue one side of an ebony strip and put its dry side against the glued side of the rosewood. Glue one side of a satinwood strip and put its dry side against the glued side of the ebony. Repeat the procedure with all the strips, alternating rosewood, ebony, satinwood, ebony, rosewood, ebony, and so on until the full 36-inch width has been made up.

Now lay the metal bars on the sides of the assembly and push them against the glued strips, topping everything with the second metal plate and the second plywood clamping board. Put a handscrew at each corner of the assembly, tightening it just enough to barely hold the whole together. Now put a bar clamp across the whole assembly, clamping the metal bars against the strips between the boards. This bar clamp should be centered in the length of the assembly. Turn the assembly over and apply two more bar clamps, one near each end, and pull these up tightly. Now tighten the handscrews to hold everything flat and true. Put more handscrews in between the bar clamps, two on each side opposite each other, and reaching almost to the center of the clamping boards. Allow the glue to cure overnight; then, after removing the clamps, lightly sand the surfaces to remove any spilled glue that may remain on them. If no excess glue has been expressed onto the surfaces, do not sand at all. You do not want to reduce the thickness any more than absolutely necessary. The top and bottom sheets of ebony veneer may now be coated with glue, and the whole returned to the clamping boards or put into the veneer press just the same as though you were crossbanding or face-and-back veneering. After the assembly has cured over night, one edge can be jointed true and the whole sliced into the strips described before.

Inlay border strips are very useful for setting off the central panel veneer from the outer border frame veneer. If a panel is not to be framed, an inlay strip may or may not be used, depending upon individual taste, but in general the inlay strip is used only in conjunction with the border frame. The exception to this usage is when the inlay strip is worked into a fancy pattern itself, which then becomes the border frame for the central panel and no mitered veneer frame is necessary. We will discuss this a bit later on.

For the average work, however, the finished panel is made up of a central matched veneer, an inlay strip all around the sides, generally set in about an inch and one-half, then bordered by a frame of veneer. The frame veneer may be either the same as the center, or, if the center is burl, butt, crotch, or other fancy figure, plain longwood grain veneer, mitered at the corners.

While it is entirely possible to make up the complete panel in tape and glue it to the core as one assembly, it is much easier to put in the inlay and the border frame after the panel has been made up. Assembling all the veneers under tape would require exquisite care in the making and taping of all the joints, since the center, inlay, and border must be made up to the exact final size of the panel. I am going to leave this method to those of my readers who like to experiment and putter around doing things for amusement and knowledge, and describe the easier way of framing and inlaying after the panel has been through the press.

Select a strip which is compatible with the inside panel and the outside frame, one with an outer border lighter or darker than the wood it is going up against. You do not want to show contrast as much as a dividing line that will set off the main veneer, and at the same time allow the material of the inlay strip to be clearly seen.

Inlay strips which are made with a continuous running band in the center, having no block or other design in it, are simple enough to use. Just miter the corners to make a good square joint and glue them in place. Inlay strips, however, which are made up of small sections to form a design, color pattern, or contrast, must be treated differently. Nothing is more unsightly than a table top or the top of a chest, otherwise beautifully crafted out of choice material, with a fancy inlay strip set around the edges and no attention paid to the matching of the pattern within the strip itself. It is the rule, rather than the exception, for commercial furniture to be inlayed simply by starting at one corner, running down a side to the next corner, mitering that joint and continuing on around the table using the inlay strip as it comes for its full length. Half of a light block in the strip may be mitered against a whole dark block, or any old combination is good enough. The pattern is not continuous, the woods at the joints clash with one another, and the whole effect is that of sloppy craftsmanship, which it is.

It takes a good bit of manipulation and common sense to properly inlay a border strip. First, if the edge being worked is longer than one strip of inlay, then the inlay must be set in two lengths (or more) with an exact match line just the same as if it were veneer. The easiest way to do this is to make a mark exactly in the center of the panel edge, dividing the space in half, if two strips of inlay will cover the edge—or divide the space in thirds or fourths according to the number of inlay strips it will take to complete the run along the edge. When one strip of inlay will fill the space lay it in place and look at the overlapping ends. If the pattern in the inlay comes out in a good match at the corners (which are going to be mitered), then all you have to do is miter the ends of each strip and you are ready to glue it in place.

If the pattern does not match, then you have to adjust the strips until it does. This adjustment is done, not at the corners of the inlay strips, as might be expected, but at the joint at the center-line. For an inlay requiring more than one strip for all four sides of the panel, pairs must be matched and mitered on all four

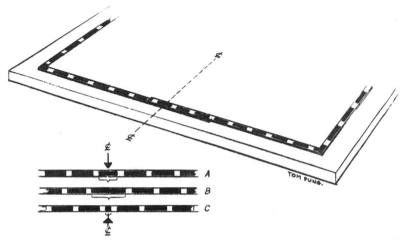

Corners are mitered first and the inlay strips overlapped at the center of the panel. The strips are then matched and cut through at the center line so that the inlay pattern is continuous and symmetrical. A, B, and C illustrate three different ways of doing this.

corners *before* you attempt the match at the center-line. Holding paired strips at right-angles to each other, move them one way or another until the corners make a good pattern match. While moving these strips, attention must be paid to the fact that the other end of each strip must reach beyond the center-line marked on the panel. After a good corner match is achieved, mark the strips carefully at the center-lines on the panel and square off the ends at this point. Theoretically, after you have made a match at one corner, all the remaining corners can be cut to duplicate the first and the inlay strips will fall in place. In practice, however, this rarely happens; each corner should be matched up the same as the first one. One thing you have the advantage of, though, is a guide for the last three corners. After the first one has been cut to fit, the *miters* can be transferred to the opposite strips. Then, matching the mitered corners, the center joint can be marked and squared off. The very slight irregularity that might occur at the center will go completely unnoticed, since the critical focal point is at the mitered corners.

To prepare the panel for receiving inlay borders, first decide whether you are going to frame the panel as well as inlay it; if you do not plan to frame it, it is simply a matter of determining just how far inside the edge you want to put the inlay strip. Then select a cutter for the router that is the exact size of the inlay and rout a groove right around the four sides to a depth slightly less than the thickness of the inlay strip. The strip should not be set flush with

Routing a complicated channel for inlays is a slow, painstaking job, and great care must be taken to start and stop the router within the margins laid out on the work.

the surface of the panel; it should protrude about the thickness of a piece of paper to allow for sanding down flush. The corners of the groove run in with a router will have to be cut square by hand with a sharp chisel. If the inlay strip has a width that cannot be matched in the router cutter, then a smaller cutter should be used and the groove run twice, one setting for the inside edge of the inlay strip and the second for the outside width.

After the grooves have been run and the inlays matched and mitered, glue can be run into the grooves. Apply the glue spar-

The corners of the routed grooves must be squared carefully with a very sharp chisel.

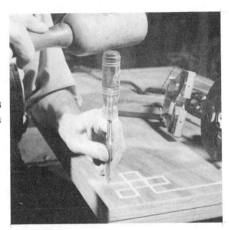

ingly, since the excess glue will be forced out onto the surface of the panel. Then set the inlays in the groove and hold them in place with short lengths of masking tape stretched across them. Lay pressure bars covered with a strip of waxed paper on top of the inlays, making sure that the bars are tight against each other at the corners so the mitered joints are covered, and clamp up the whole with handscrews or C-clamps. If you place the clamping

Be sparing of glue in the channels because the excess has no place to go when the panel is clamped up.

125

The inlay strip can be held tight against the panel with the use of thumbtacks until the border is cut and fitted.

bars around the panel with the end of one bar butted up against the side of the adjacent one, they will cover the inlay strips completely and the bars can project beyond the edges of the panel without having to be accurately cut to length.

If the panel is going to be framed as well as inlayed, then no groove is cut for the inlay. Instead, using the widest flat-ended cutter you have, set it to cut at the location for the inside edge of the inlay strip, and rout off all the veneer from this line outward. Since the average frame border is about 1½ inches wide, and the inlay around ¼ inch wide, you will be routing off not less than 1¾ inches from all the sides of the panel. The depth should be just less than the thickness of the veneer used for the framing. Always use a scrap piece of wood for a test setting of the router before going at the panel.

After the edge has been routed, the inlay strips are matched to

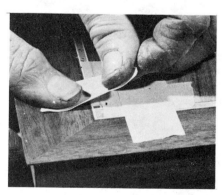

Pull the tape across both the inlay and the border right near the miters to act as hinges when applying the glue.

fit snugly against the veneer, and taped in position to the panel. The masking tape should be placed so that it does not overlap the outer edges of the inlay strips, since the framing veneer must be put into place at this point. The framing veneer is cut into strips a little wider than the routed space alloted to them on the panel, and the ends mitered accurately to fit all around the panel tight against the inlay strips. Now masking tape can be put over both

The border and the inlay are lifted together in order to spread the glue.

the framing strips and the inlay strips and left in place until the edges are glued. Lift up the veneer and the inlay on one edge and spread the panel with glue underneath them. Drop them back down on top of the glue and stick a short length of masking tape over the edge of the veneer, pulling it around the bottom of the

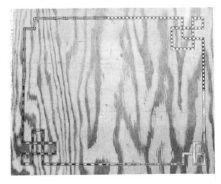

A scrap board may be used for a pattern from which to set the router when you make the inlays. The most-used corners can be laid out this way, to save setting-up time.

127

panel to hold all in place while you work the remaining three edges. Repeat this performance with each edge, working right around the panel. Clamping bars wide enough to cover the framing veneer and the inlay strip together should be put in place and clamped with handscrews or large C-clamps.

When framing with veneers that are soft and porous, such as mahogany, primavera, and avodire, you might have to put masking tape directly across the mitered joints to keep them pulled up tightly until the clamps are in place. Otherwise the veneers may suck up the glue and curl so much that they will not go back into place under the clamping bar. Hardwoods are not usually prone to this trouble.

The overlapping edges of the framing veneer may be trimmed off almost flush with the edges of the panel with the same router and cutter used on the edging board. This will leave only a few thousandths of an inch of veneer standing, which may be easily sanded off flush with the edges. Be careful when you use the edging router that you do not tear the veneer at the corners. It is best to cut in toward the center of the panel from one corner, then go back and start at the other corner, trimming the edge to meet the first cut.

Fancy figures made with the inlay strips are sometimes useful, although they are not generally in good taste when used in conjunction with a highly figured veneer; the veneer pattern together with the pattern of the inlay strip makes the completed panel too "busy." A turn at the corners or even a knot may well be put in when the veneer used on the piece is plain and not highly figured. This application is almost always used when there is no frame around the edges, the intricacy of the inlay being enough to accent the panel.

If a knot or other complicated pattern is inlaid, and if it is repeated in more than one corner, then, as you make each different setting on the router for grooving the panel, cut that same section in all corners before going on to the next cut. You should draw the entire pattern you intend to make accurately and legibly

A trouble light laid on the work will provide illumination right at the cutter.

on the panel. Particularly important are lines marking the ends of the grooves; rout just to these, stopping exactly on the line each time. If it is difficult to see the cutter as you are working, lay a trouble light on the work, faced so that it shines under the router motor and illuminates the inside around the spindle.

An even safer method is to set up stops. On a scrap of wood, clamp another small board near one end, then run the router down until it meets the stop. Brush away all the shavings, then with a square and a sharp pencil, make a line across the board just touching the end of the groove. Measuring from this line to the stop gives you the dimension for setting up the stop on your work. If, for example, the distance was 3 inches, then, after drawing the pattern carefully on the panel, clamp a stop exactly 3 inches from the end of the groove and rout until the machine touches the stop. The stop will have to be moved for each cut, and this will slow down the work. But you shouldn't be in a hurry anyway, and the use of a stop will make the cuts much more accurate and easy to make.

12

FINISHING VENEERS

Finishing veneered work is different from finishing panels made out of solid lumber, in that you have only a very thin surface to work with. If you work too long in one spot, there is an excellent chance of sanding right through the face veneer and exposing the crossbanding. This, of course, ruins that panel and you have your work to do all over again. If the panel has already been made up into furniture, you can get into real trouble.

For this reason, unless you are a master hand at using belt sanders, you should never use such a tool on the surface of the panel. I have used them for so many years that they are second nature to me; I automatically pick up the belt sander when I have a panel to finish. But they are dangerous and I cannot honestly recommend them.

The dangers of this fast cutting tool are several. Perhaps the worst one is that, as you sand, you may not even be aware of a tilting of the tool. It may be only a slight tilting, yet it is enough to cut gullies into the face veneer, often right through it to the crossbanding. It takes a fraction of a second to do so, and there is really no way to correct the damage, once done. There is also the danger of sanding right through the face veneer at the start and stop of the runs. The way you use a belt sander is to allow the machine to run itself down the length of the panel, then you pull it back and start over again. A momentary hesitation at the far end of the stroke and at the beginning of the stroke more than doubles the sanding time in those areas in relation to that on the rest of the panel. Before you are aware of it, you suddenly find that you are down to the crossbanding at both ends of the panel. If you do use a belt sander, the only thing I can tell you to help reduce the danger is to use the widest one you can possibly find. The width will tend to stabilize the machine somewhat, and lessen the chance of its tilting and gullying at the sides.

The next fastest cutting sander is the rotary machine. The disadvantage of this one is that it sometimes makes a multitude of scratch rings the diameter of the rotational stroke of the pad. These can be difficult to remove from the face of the work if the face veneer is soft and the rings have been cut deeply. The most common cause of such rings is too much pressure on the machine. The weight of the machine should be the only pressure; you merely guide it. Also, when sanding with successive grades of paper, a single grain from a coarser grade of paper might remain on the surface of the work, to be picked up when you start to sand with the next finer grade; this will work havoc on the veneer, cutting deep ridges into the surface. It is good practice to get into the habit of using a brush—frequently—as you sand; dust off the surface of the panel thoroughly as you go along, and also brush off the sandpaper on the machine. Never lay the machine down on the sanding pad. You can pick up all sorts of foreign abrasives which can cause trouble. Always lay the machine down on its side when you rest it or finish sanding with it. Also, always get into the habit of slapping the sheet of sandpaper against the edge of the workbench, or your leg, to dislodge loose particles before you put it on the machine. I regularly give a few strokes with the sander on a scrap piece of wood before I put it to work on the panel. This further dislodges large grains and foreign particles that have stuck to the paper.

A rotary sander will take the surface down quite easily, but quite a bit more slowly than a belt sander. However, it is so much safer to use that it should be the machine of your choice, especially when you start veneering. Remember that with any sander when you run over the edge, you will invariably round the edge off. You can avoid this by sizing your stroke so that the machine runs up to, and overhangs slightly, each edge of the panel, but pull it back when not more than a third of the sanding pad has run over the edge. Keeping the larger area of the pad on the surface of the panel helps you hold the machine flat.

With a reciprocal or straight-line sander, as with a belt sander, always sand in the direction of the grain. Even when a panel has been framed and inlaid with a border strip, on the first or rough sanding run with the grain right out to both ends, sanding across the frame. Later, when the finish sanding is done, you can stop short at the frame. Then, with a block and fine sandpaper, hand-sand the frame all around going with the grain of the frame itself and not touching the panel part. This must be done anyway, to sand to the miters at each corner. The block should be held at a 45 degree angle, and run up just to the miter joint. If you cannot control your stroke so as not to overrun the joint, clamp a stop-block at the corner and sand up to the stop, moving the block each time you go to another corner.

When using a rotary sander, it is not as important to watch the grain of the veneer, since the rotary motion precludes the possibility of following the grain anyway. The use of a rotary sander must always be followed by a final hand-sanding to remove any rings left by the machine.

Sandpaper comes in many grades. About the coarsest grade to be used on veneers is 100 or 2/0. This paper is used for the first sanding—to remove the paper tapes after the panel comes from the press, and to remove all saw marks on the very hard-sawn veneers. Grade 120 or 3/0 is the coarsest that should be used on sanding machines. The type of paper best to use is open-coat, and the grit that is best for veneer work is silicon carbide, although garnet is also good. You should avoid using the old style flint paper. The grit is too uneven on this paper, it fills too readily in use, and it is difficult to get a fine enough surface to do really fine finishing with it.

Sometimes sanding a panel can be speeded up a bit by scraping the surface first, to remove all marks made by the slicing knife or saw when the veneer was cut. This can be done with impunity only on very hard woods such as ebony or rosewood, when the grain is not curly or highly figured, or on snakewood, tulipwood, and others of the same degree of hardness. A hook scraper can be used if it is kept razor-sharp and a light pressure applied when using. The safest method of scraping is to use a flat cabinet scraper, again kept very sharp and used with light strokes. With a lot of experience, you can scrape an ebony panel, for instance, to the point where you need only give it the final sanding with the finest grade of paper. To try to do this much scraping with other than hardwoods is merely asking for trouble, and to scrape any veneer with a curly grain, highly ornate figure, or knots in the surface is compounding the danger. Nothing will pull a knot out of a panel faster than passing a hook scraper over it. Even changes of direction in the grain cause patches to pull up. Some of the mahoganies, even when worked with a cabinet scraper, will "fur" up so badly that you have to sand halfway through the veneer to get back to solid wood.

All the first sanding should be done on the individual panels before the furniture is assembled. The final finishing stages are done after assembly. These consist of two more sandings. After the piece has been assembled and is ready to be finished, it should be sanded with 4/0 finishing paper, preferably silicon carbide, and then thoroughly dusted. I keep a small hand vacuum cleaner in my shop and go over every piece carefully between sandings to make certain that every grain of the coarse grit has been removed before going down to the next finer paper. One grain is all you need to score the surface of your work very badly.

The final finish sanding is done with 6/0 or 7/0 finishing paper if the veneer is a soft wood. If it is a hardwood veneer, then the final stage should be done with 10/0 paper. Never allow the surface of these fine papers to fill with dust. Frequently, while sanding, either by hand or with an electric sander, knock out the

133

surface of the paper to clear it of packing. The two final stages of sanding must be done with the grain, without running over the border strips or framing if they are present. These should be sanded separately following their own grain.

Thoroughly dust the work after the final sanding, vacuuming it if possible. Then, with a clean cloth wet with lacquer-thinner wipe down all the surfaces to pick up any remaining dust or sand grains. The lacquer-thinner will evaporate almost immediately, and will not affect any of the finishes you are going to use.

For woods like teak, the best way to finish is with oil. If you want a light finish, use plain clear mineral oil (the same used as a laxative), and apply it generously to the entire surface with a brush or small sponge. Allow the oil to soak into the surface for about five minutes, then wipe off the excess with dry cloths. A second application about a week after the first will suffice to make a permanent finish on the article, which may then be put into service. Perhaps once a year a light application of the oil, well rubbed down, will keep it in top shape.

For dark finishes on oiled teak use boiled linseed oil instead of the mineral oil. This oil actually chars the wood, and the length of time you leave the oil on the surface before wiping off the excess determines the amount of darkness imparted to the teak. For this reason, it is necessary to make certain that all parts of the piece of furniture are treated for the same length of time. It is not a good idea to put the oil over the entire surface before starting to wipe it off. Rather, coat one panel, let it stand for the desired time then wipe it off, proceeding to the next. The oil remaining just under the surface of the wood will continue the darkening process after the surface has been wiped off. So do not wait until the exact dark shade has been achieved, or you will end with a too-dark panel. Experience will tell you just how long to let the oil remain on the surface before removing the excess, but I have found that not more than two or three minutes will be enough.

One caution: a rag soaked with linseed oil and thrown down in a heap will start to generate heat within minutes, and can—and often does—burst into flame within an hour or so, taking with it whatever it was tossed upon, if not the entire shop! So never throw a linseed oil-soaked rag away until it has thoroughly dried. Open them out completely and hang them over a line individually, leaving them there until they are stiff and dry, which may take a week. Then they can be put in the trash can, provided it is metal and has a cover. Even when dry, they should not be thrown into a shop waste barrel where sawdust and shavings are likely to be deposited.

Not too many woods take well to an oiled finish. Teak is a natural, and I never finish it any other way. Rosewood and ebony look well with an oiled surface when the oil used is mineral oil. They turn nearly black under linseed oil, and most of the beauty of their grain is lost. Walnut also takes oil very well, and in certain instances an oiled finish is to be preferred. In general, if the wood is naturally oily, it should do well with an oiled finish; if it is dry, oil would alter its appearance enough to spoil the beauty of the grain.

For fine rare veneers, the best way to finish is with a clear lacquer, no filler and no stain. This would be called open-pore finish. The use of clear lacquer and no filler allows the natural grain and texture of the wood to stand out. It is unthinkable to make a piece out of some fine veneer and then stain it! The reason for selecting these veneers in the first place is because of their natural grains and colors. To go to all the trouble of making them up into furniture, then filling the grain with a paste, and dying everything with an artificial coloring agent seems to be defeating the purpose.

The only lacquer finish I ever use is Satinlac. This is made by the United States Plywood Corporation, and it is truly a marvelous finishing medium. It is easily applied with a soft brush, dries fast, and practically disappears after drying and rubbing, letting the wood appear natural. It does not influence the colors of the woods, except possibly to brighten them a bit. Not less than four coats should be given each surface, and preferably six. Each coat should be well brushed in, especially the first one, and given

135

plenty of time to dry. The first coat will dry completely within an hour or so, depending upon the temperature of the air and the humidity within the room. After drying and between coats, very lightly sand the surface with 8/0 or 10/0 finishing paper and a hand block. Do not use a machine for sanding between coats. Each coat will take a little longer to dry, since the porosity of the wood will be lessened by virtue of being filled with lacquer. This makes the drying entirely dependent upon the evaporation of the volatile solvents into the air, rather than the combination of evaporation and absorption into the wood.

After the final coat, sandpaper should not be used. Instead the surface is now rubbed down with a pad of 3/0 or 4/0 steel wool. Turn the pad frequently to present a clean unfilled surface to the lacquer. The surface should be steel-wooled evenly all over. After that it should be thoroughly dusted with a brush and, if possible, vacuumed to remove the splinters of steel which will insist on remaining packed into corners and around edges.

Two coats of wax may now be applied—preferably a hard paste wax—and well rubbed down. The surface will take a soft shine which brings out the grain and colors of the veneers and is practically stain proof. Maintenance of this type of finish requires another coat of wax at intervals of six months to a year, depending on the amount of handling the article is subjected to. A table top, for instance, will need more frequent waxing than a dresser top.

Varnish may be used on veneered work, if you prefer the more leisurely finishing time possible with this material. Because it is slow drying, the room in which you work must be absolutely dust free. Before you start to varnish, the floor should be swept and mopped with a wet mop. Do not wear the same clothes in which you sanded the work, but change to fresh clothing to insure that you do not carry dust into the room. This also applies to your shoes. Walk slowly and carefully to avoid stirring up any dust that may remain on the floor.

Use the best varnish you can obtain, and try to get one that is designated as "water-clear." Some varnishes, if they are not yellow in the can, will turn quite a deep yellow shortly after application, thus obscuring much of the grain and natural color of the veneer. Three coats of varnish should be applied, and each coat worked in well in the direction of the grain. Allow ample time for drying between coats. Following the directions on the can should insure a good job. But even if it is not stated in the directions, I recommend that the first coat be cut about 20 per cent with turpentine or paint thinner before application. The remaining two coats can then be applied full strength as it comes from the can.

Not less than twenty-four hours after application, the surface should be lightly sanded with 3/0 or 4/0 opencoat finishing paper, then wiped off with a clean cloth to remove all loose matter. The last coat is rubbed with pumice and oil, pumice and water, rottenstone and oil, or rottenstone and water. The differences between these materials is that pumice is coarser and cuts more rapidly than rottenstone, and water cuts faster than oil whatever medium is used with it. Perhaps the best method is to use pumice and water for a light rubbing to even out the surface and remove any blemishes that might have occured, dust spots, and hairs. For the final rubbing use rottenstone and oil; this will yield a very smooth, soft luster which may then be waxed and polished with a soft cloth.

The pads used for rubbing down varnish and lacquer may be made of pieces of 3/4-inch plywood or regular lumber, of a size that can be conveniently held in the hand. The blocks should be faced with a good quality of felt. An old hat will supply felt of an excellent quality sufficient to cover several rubbing blocks.

Never use the same block for different rubbing compounds. Keep each block for use with the material you started with, and mark the blocks so that you do not lose track of them. It is impossible to completely remove one rubbing compound from a felt pad so you could use it with another.

Several modern finishes have found their way into the home shop to be used on furniture. Among them are the clear vinyls, clear epoxy, and acrylic resin lacquer. The vinyl is easily applied with a soft brush. The epoxy may prove a bit difficult because it is so sticky; but the finish will justify the extra trouble. It is practically damage-proof, dries with a high gloss, and is self-leveling. To apply, use a stiff brush and cover small areas at a time. When applied properly in a dust-free atmosphere, an epoxy finish should not require rubbing to produce a smooth surface.

Acrylic resin lacquer cannot be brushed on because it dries too quickly. It is available in pressure spray cans, and in this form is quite easy to use. Some of the vinyls are also available in pressure cans.

Whenever possible, it is always best to spray fast-drying finishes rather than to try to brush them on. For that matter, any finish is more evenly applied with a spray gun than it could be with a brush.

A finish that has found some application, especially for the tops of coffee tables, end tables, and similar pieces of furniture, is hot lacquer. This lacquer is much the same as the ordinary kind used on furniture, but it is put on with a spray gun having a heated container to keep the lacquer quite hot during application. The heat thins the lacquer until it runs almost as easily as water. Thus, it levels itself perfectly before it cools, making it unnecessary to sand between coats, and it dries very rapidly. Layer after layer is built up on the leveled surface of the panel, until there is an actual thickness of lacquer. The surface is glass-smooth and brilliantly glossy, and the thickness gives a depth to the surface of the work that sets off the grain remarkably well. The surface always appears to be liquid when you look at it sideways.

Recently, hot lacquer has come to be the usual finish applied to the doors of kitchen cabinets, because the smoothness of the surface does not collect grease and dirt readily and is much easier to wipe clean. It is not difficult to do yourself if you are a good hand at spray-lacquering, but the equipment is costly and takes up a lot of shop space. For the occasional piece you would want to finish in this manner, it might be better to hire it done. You will find firms that specialize in this kind of finish listed in the yellow pages of the telephone book.

13

REPAIRING VENEERS AND VENEERED WORK

Once in a while it is necessary to make some kind of repair to a veneered surface, which was damaged either during production or after it has been completed and is in use. It is much easier to repair damages which were sustained while the piece was in work than it is to do so after finishing. With the increased popularity of pre-finished plywood panelling for rooms, various manufacturers have put out putty sticks for filling the nail holes. These are wax crayons, colored to match a great variety of veneers, and they can be used to advantage to repair small nicks and blemishes. However, the color of wood will change slightly with the application of the finishing medium; the color in the putty stick will remain unchanged. If the repair were made before finishing, matching the stick to the raw veneer, it could very well magnify the blemish, rather than hide it. Also, lacquers and varnishes may dissolve the wax and pull it out of the nick, at the same time leaving a smear on the surface of the panel. It is, therefore, best to use the sticks after the piece has been lacquered or varnished. This way you can match the color of the finished veneer, rather than that of the raw wood.

Sometimes a chip of veneer will be pulled from a piece of furniture, usually from an edge or an end of a chest or table. The edges of drawers are often thus damaged, and they can be repaired right

The drawer opening makes a convenient holder for the work while the glue cures.

in place by letting the opening they fit into act as a holder for the drawer while the repair strip is being clamped in glue. The damaged strip can either be planed or chiselled off and a new one applied with one of the quick-setting glues like Presto-Set.

It is always best to take the entire strip off and replace it with an entirely new one, instead of trying to match the grain and color of the old strip if the piece has been in service for some time. Unless you make the habit of saving trimmings and pieces from identical sheets of veneer each time you make a cabinet, there is a very poor possibility of ever being able to find just the same color match for a later repair. One of the things I have gotten into the habit of doing is to put aside small pieces of each of the different veneers that go into the making of a cabinet. Then, when the cabinet has been assembled and finished, I put all the scraps into a strong envelope and tack or tape it to the back or the bottom of the cabinet for safe-keeping. The scraps are out of the way and yet accessible whenever needed, and this little trick will save you many a headache trying to match up the grains or figures. The color is secondary in making a small repair, since the patch can be colored to match the rest of the aged veneer if necessary. The big thing is to be able to match the general grain size and shapes, or the figure, if the original veneer was fancy.

Of course, if the damage is to the surface of a panel instead of an edge, you cannot very easily strip the panel to re-veneer it. Here all your ingenuity is brought to play in matching up the figure. As I mentioned earlier in this volume, punches are made for repairing veneers on the surfaces of panels. These come in several sizes and shapes, each shape different from another, because all the punches are handmade in Europe and the shapes are individual. Actually, the shape of the cutout is not important; the main idea is to break a straight line to lead the eye away from the patch.

If, for instance, you made a repair by simply cutting out a rectangle or a square, or even a circle, and inlaying a new section of veneer in place, whenever you looked at that panel, the first thing to meet your eye would be the lines of the repair. When a veneer punch is used, the wavy and irregular line of the repair blends so well with the figure in the veneer that the patch is virtually invisible and may never be seen unless you point it out. As a matter of fact, I have made repairs at times that I was later unable to find myself, and spent many minutes examining the surface of the panel until finally I was able to make out the faint line of the joints.

A selection of four or five punches will suffice for all the repairs you will ever need to do, since it is possible to make two or more punch-outs overlapping each other. When this is done, each punch-cut must be made and the piece set in before the overlapping cut is made. More of this a little later on in this chapter.

In general, the fancier the figure of a veneer, the easier it is to repair it, since the very wildness of the figure will tend to conceal the outline of the repair. It is this fact that was taken in consideration when these punches were designed. Unfortunately, the punches are hard to find in this country. The only firm I know of that has them is H. L. Wild, 510 East 11th Street, New York, N.Y. This company always carries a complete assortment of the repair punches and does a mail order business.

The punches should be kept good and sharp, and this may be done by filing the edges *on the outside only* until very sharp. Any slight alteration of shape is unimportant, since the shape is arbitrary to begin with, and the same punch is used to cut out the

141

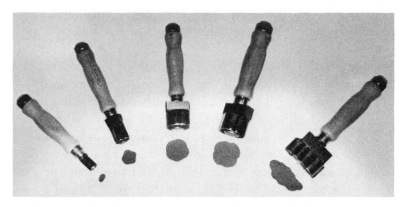

Five useful sizes of veneer punches and the shapes they make for repairing.

blemish and cut the patch. Avoid all sharp corners when filing and try to keep them rounded.

A repair punch has a spring-loaded ejector in the center of the cutting area to push out the piece of veneer after punching. This, of course, operates only when cutting the repair chip; not when punching the defect on a veneered panel.

To use, select a punch that is large enough to cover completely the injury or defect in the panel you are repairing. Position the punch over the defect and press it down tightly enough to over-come the tension of the ejector spring and bring the cutting edge in contact with the work. Then give the punch a sharp blow with a heavy hammer or light maul. Try to drive it through the face veneer with one stroke, rather than with several lighter strokes. This will avoid the danger of moving the punch during successive strokes. The material inside the punch-cut may now be removed with a sharp chisel, taking care to lift out only the face veneer and not to cut through into the crossbanding. Great care should be taken not to mar the edges of the punch-cut with the chisel when removing the waste. A woodcarver's skew chisel is the best tool for this work, since the skew allows you to get right up into a sharp corner while the cutting edge of the chisel is within full view of

142

the user. If you do not have a skew chisel and are going to buy one for this work, get one with a shallow spoon bend.

After cleaning out the area of the punch the piece of veneer that is to be used for the repair is held against the site, and moved about to obtain the best match of the figure or grain. Pencil a rough outline on the veneer to indicate the position of the punch for cutting the repair chip. The veneer is now laid on a block of end-grain wood, preferably maple or birch, although any close grained hard wood will do. Position the punch according to your pencilled guide lines and press the punch down until it is tightly in contact with the veneer. A good blow with the heavy hammer or maul should cut the chip out in one stroke. The spring ejector should pop the chip out of the punch without splitting the veneer.

If the veneer is dry and splitty, it should be slightly dampened either by wiping it with a cloth wet with water, or dampened with the veneer flexiblizing solution as discussed in chapter seven (p. 78). It would not be necessary to soak the veneer in the solution as you do for working burls; just dampen both sides a bit before punching the chip. In extreme cases, with veneers that splinter at a touch, thuya and amboyna burls being a couple of such woods, it may be found necessary to paste a strip of paper veneering tape on the surface of the veneer before punching the chip in order to hold the wood together under the shock of punching. When this is necessary, do not remove the paper before using the chip but glue it into place, then sand the paper off the surface when re-finishing the panel. Of course, the paper on the surface of the veneer will make it difficult for you to see what you are doing when you punch the chip, so accurate guide lines should be made on the veneer which will project out from under the paper, in order to assist in positioning the punch. After selecting the best position for matching the repair, two lines can be drawn through the area at right angles to each other, across the middle of the desired area crossways and lengthways. When these lines are drawn, consideration

143

must be given to the lengthwise and crosswise axes of the punch in order to be able to position it accurately.

Sometimes veneer repair punches can be used to repair damage done on things other than panels. A fancy door, for instance, which was bored incorrectly for the lock, may often be saved by using the punches to replace veneer around the holes. If the holes have been bored through the door, the veneer punch should be used and the excess veneer removed from the punched area before the holes are filled. The filling is then put in flush with the bottom of the cavity made for the repair. It would be very difficult to chisel out the plug which would present its end grain to the surface if the plug were put in before the punch was used.

A large area may be replaced with veneer punches, up to a limit, of course, by overlapping the punch-cuts. This is a long and tedious process, and should be used only when the veneer being worked is of great enough beauty or value to warrant the expenditure of time and trouble. As many as three or four cuts may be made to cover the entire flawed area in the work. The first cut is made and the patch punched out and inserted in its proper position. If the panel has been glued up, which really is the best time to patch with veneering punches, the first cutout is made and the patch glued in. The next cut is then made, with the punch overlapping in any position that is convenient to cover the greatest portion of the remaining flaw, and the second patch matched up, punched, and glued into place. Continue in this manner until all the flawed portion of the veneer has been patched. Naturally, multiple punch repairs are recommended only when the figure of the face veneer is fancy enough to conceal the large number of joint lines. Such repairs could not be well hidden on a panel of straight grained veneer; but then, this type of veneer would not really be worth the time and trouble to make compound repairs, to begin with.

Many times the edge parts of a knot are sound enough in the sheet of veneer, but the centers are missing, either due to rot in the tree, or to the fact that the center "eye" dried and shrank free of

144

the rest of the knot, dropping out as the sheets were handled in the factory. Look on the salesroom floor around such a flitch to see if there are a lot of small round pieces of veneer. If there are, take them, since the chance that these are the "eyes" is a good one, and they can be used to repair the sheets you buy. Otherwise, buy several additional sheets for matching repair material in case of need. Then, when you are ready to glue up your panels, each knot can be repaired with the use of veneer repair punches and the spare sheets. Try to punch out the repair piece from the same position in the extra sheets as the spot you are attempting to repair. Naturally, the exact spot cannot be used, because if it were sound, you would not have to repair the veneer to begin with. Use

There are exactly 40 veneer punch repairs in this magnificent quarter-matched stump walnut panel. Can you find them?

145

the intact sheets instead. But each knot may have a slightly different color or texture, so repair each place from the closest spot in the extra sheets.

Quite often, when buying walnut burls and crotch veneers already matched you will find multiple punch repairs made in them. Such veneers are often made up into matched sheets, taped, ready to use as a face veneer for small table tops or chests. Practically never will you come across such a sheet without at least several repair patches.

Blistering and tenting are two troubles that sometimes occur in veneered panels after the completed item of furniture has been in service for some time. Blistering is generally caused by insufficient glue in spots under the face veneer, although it can also be the result of poor patching in the core panel. If the surfacing putty used in patching the core did not adhere very well, the whole patch, usually a round knot hole in the core veneer, can loosen, carrying the crossbanding and the face veneer with it. This type of blister is harder to repair than one caused by not enough glue under the face veneer, because you must get glue down under the face veneer, the crossbanding, and the surfacing putty patch.

The best way to do this is to drill a small hole through the veneer into the cavity beneath, then inject glue with a glue syringe or a large hypodermic syringe with a heavy gauge needle. Not too much glue should be injected, because the excess will be forced under the already-glued veneer. If this happens, your repair may simply cause more damage, by loosening the surrounding veneer to make room for the excess glue injected into the loose spot. If a small quantity of glue gets under the surfacing putty patch, it will hold the patch in place and tighten the blister, even though the entire sub-surface is not completely coated. After the glue is injected, the spot must be put under pressure until the glue sets. If the repair is on a panel this is simply a matter of returning the panel to the veneer press, but if the panel has been made into a piece of furniture, as is often the case before a blister develops, clamping may present quite a problem. Sometimes the entire cabinet may be clamped between pressure cauls in order to get the pressure on the loose spot. If the blister is near enough to an open edge a large handscrew might do the job.

Sometimes, however, you will find it impossible either to clamp the entire cabinet or to use clamps at all. Here you must improvise. A good way I have found to do this is to make use of the ceiling and an automobile jack as a jury clamp, to apply the necessary pressure, following this procedure.

Place the cabinet on a level part of the shop or garage floor; try it in different positions until you are sure that all the feet are solidly planted and the cabinet will not be wracked out of true when pressure is applied. Cover the repaired spot with a sheet of waxed paper to contain the glue if it oozes and on this place a pressure caul. Now, erect your makeshift clamp on top of this: put the jack—preferably a scissors jack—on the caul; on the jack stand a length of 4 x 4 lumber, long enough to reach nearly to the ceiling; between this upright and the ceiling wedge two or three thicknesses of plywood, not less than 2 feet square so as to distribute the pressure evenly against the ceiling. Then, carefully raise the jack until all is tight and secure, and leave the cabinet under pressure over night until the glue has cured.

If the blister being repaired is over a hollow part of the cabinet, then bridging must be placed within the piece to avoid distorting or even snapping the joints. This can be scrap lumber cut to fit exactly from the top to the bottom of the cavity, and slid into place directly under the repair spot. If the cabinet is on feet or on a toe-kick, then a short bridge must be also installed directly under the main bridge, reaching from under the bottom of the cabinet to the floor. Unless these bridges are placed before all is put under pressure, there is a better than good chance of snapping the cabinet apart when the jack is tightened. Remember when raising the jack that it was designed to lift a heavy car or truck, and a very little cranking goes a long way in applying pressure. You can actually rip out a ceiling with this rig unless you use discretion.

The same method of jacking for pressure can be used between

walls instead of from floor to ceiling, if the repair is being made on the side or end of a cabinet, and it is unhandy to tip the piece to use a vertical rig.

The small hole made when drilling for the glue syringe may now be filled and the surface refinished if necessary. In straight-grain veneers, it is often possible to make a cut with a sharp razor-blade knife instead of drilling a hole. One half of the blister is then lifted up and glue slid within the loose cavity, repeated with the other side and then clamped in place. When the repair is made by slitting, it is often unnecessary to do anything else to the surface; the slit will disappear when the blister is clamped down in place.

Tenting is really the same as blistering, except it occurs at the edge of a panel, and generally along the line of matching two pieces of veneer. This trouble is often caused by keeping the furniture in a place that is damp. It can also be caused by setting potted plants on the surface of a veneered panel, and not being extra careful when watering. A very few drops of spilled water can ruin a veneer joint. The moisture runs under the pot or the pad upon which the pot rests and remains there for days, because it is not exposed to the air and cannot evaporate. If this area is directly over a glue joint, the glue will finally soften and allow the water to seep down under the face veneer, causing it to swell right at the joint. The result is a raised part along the joint.

Tenting cannot be repaired by the simple injection of glue and pressure, caused, as it is, by swelling. If pressure were applied, you would merely fracture the veneer for the length of the tent, and glue it back down as an overlap on itself. Since the swelling is caused by moisture, the first step is to dry out the veneer at the point of the tent. This can be done by placing a warm iron on a thick pad of newspaper or blotting paper over the swelling. Under no circumstance should the iron be allowed to become really hot. A good steady warmth is all that is necessary. If you have an iron that cannot be controlled accurately, then the best thing to do is to lay a heating pad on the surface, on low or medium heat, and leave it there until the veneer has been thoroughly dried. Sometimes this may take several days, depending on the amount of finish on the surface of the cabinet. After the veneer has dried, it should shrink back into place. At this time, glue can be injected under the loose tent and the whole clamped as in the case of a blister, using the same devices described for them.

Water and liquor stains on tops of veneered furniture can generally be removed by scraping the entire top to the raw wood, sanding, and refinishing. On certain woods, however, a water stain becomes a permanent stain right through the thickness of the face veneer. Indeed, some woods actually turn black when water is spilled on them, and nothing can be done to remove the stain. If this happens, the only recourse you have in repairing the damage is to re-veneer the entire top. Since veneer cannot be glued to one side of a panel without warping that panel out of control, the new face veneer must be put in place with contact adhesive instead of with glue. The old finish must be entirely removed and the surface sanded smooth. As a matter of fact, here is the ideal place to use a belt sander, since you can cut off almost the entire thickness of the old face veneer to make room for the new layer.

Care must be taken to position the new veneer properly before putting it in contact with the cement, because the first contact is the final one with this kind of adhesive. Go over the entire surface heavily with a rolling pin, or pound it with a rubber mallet until you are sure the entire new veneer is in contact with the old surface. The edges are then hand-trimmed and the whole sanded and refinished.

14

A LIST OF COMMONLY
AVAILABLE VENEERS

Although there are literally hundreds of veneers available in the many veneer houses in this country and abroad, not all of them are good for fine cabinetry. On the following pages are listed some of the more frequently available veneers, together with their source, color, availability, and price range.

ACACIA   (Acacia spp.). *Source:* America, Europe, and India. *Color:* greenish-brown heartwood. *Availability:* rare. *Price range:* moderate.

ACCRA   (Entandrophragma, spp.). *Source:* West Africa. *Color:* rich dark red. *Availability:* rare. *Price range:* moderate.

AFRORMOSIA   (Afrormosia elata). *Other name:* Kokrodua. *Source:* West Africa. *Color:* yellow to warm brown. *Availability:* plentiful. *Price range:* moderate.

AGBA   (Gossweilerodendron balsamiferum, Harms.). *Other names:* Achi, Moboron, Pink "Mahogany". *Source:* Nigeria. *Color:*

cream white to pale cedar-brown. *Availability:* rare. *Price range:* inexpensive.

ALBARCO (Cariniana, spp.). *Other names:* Abarco, Cedro Macho, Jequitiba. *Source:* Brazil and Colombia. *Color:* light brown. *Availability:* scarce as quartered veneer. *Price range:* medium.

ALMON (Shorea almon, Scheff.). *Other name:* White Lauan. *Source:* Philippine Islands. *Color:* light straw. *Availability:* plentiful as quartered and rotary veneers. *Price range:* inexpensive.

AMARANTH (Peltogyne paniculata, Benth.). *Other names:* Amarante, Bois Violet, Morado, Palo Morado, Purpleheart, Violetwood. *Source:* Mexico, Central and South America. *Color:* deep purple heart with light grey sapwood. *Availability:* scarce as quartered and sliced veneer. *Price range:* costly.

AMBOYNA BURL (Pterocarpus indicus, Willd.). *Other name:* Kiabooca. *Source:* Borneo and the Moluccas. *Color:* rich brown, variegated to yellow and red. *Availability:* scarce as half-round veneer. *Price range:* costly. Amboyna burls are taken from the tree called Narra, but are sold under its own name as veneers. Practically no one is aware that the two so different woods are from the same tree.

ANDIROBA (Carapa guianensis, Aubl.). *Other names:* Carapa, Cedro Macho, Crabwood, Demerara. *Source:* Northern South America. *Color:* reddish-brown. *Availability:* scarce as quartered veneer. *Price range:* moderate.

151

APPLE (Pyrus malus, L.). *Source:* Europe, Asia, and the United States. *Color:* light red to reddish-brown. *Availability:* scarce as half-round veneer. *Price range:* medium.

ASH, AMERICAN (Fraxinus americana, Linn.). *Source:* Northern United States. *Color:* cream to light brown. *Availability:* plentiful, rare as burls. *Price range:* medium.

ASH, EUROPEAN (Fraxinus excelsior, Linn.). *Source:* England, France, Turkey, and Hungary. *Color:* grayish- to brownish-white. *Availability:* scarce as half-round and burls. *Price range:* costly.

ASH, JAPANESE (Fraxinus sieboldiana, Blume). *Other names:* Damo, Tamo. *Source:* Japan. *Color:* light brown to almost white. *Availability:* scarce as half-round veneer. *Price range:* costly.

ASPEN (Populus alba, Linnaeus). *Source:* Europe, Western Asia, and the United States. *Color:* white to gray. *Availability:* scarce. *Price range:* moderate to costly.

AVODIRE (Turraeanthus africana, Pell.). *Other name:* Apaya. *Source:* West Africa. *Color:* white to gold. *Availability:* plentiful. *Price range:* moderate.

AYOUS (Triplochiton scleroxylon, K. Schum.). *Other name:* Abachi, Ewowo, African Whitewood, Obeche, Samba. *Source:* West Africa. *Color:* white to pale yellow. *Availability:* plentiful. *Price range:* inexpensive.

BASSWOOD (Tilia americana, L.). *Source:* United States and Canada. *Color:* white. *Availability:* plentiful. *Price range:* inexpensive.

BEECH (Fagus grandifolia, Ehrh.). *Source:* Northern United States. *Color:* reddish-brown to white. *Availability:* plentiful. *Price range:* inexpensive.

BELLA ROSA (Anisoptera thurifera, Blume.). *Other names:* Bayott, Duali, Palosapis. *Source:* Philippine Islands. *Color:* pink to yellowish-buff. *Availability:* plentiful as quartered veneer. *Price range:* medium.

BENGE (Guibourtia aronoldiana). *Source:* West Africa. *Color:* light and dark brown stripes. *Availability:* plentiful. *Price range:* inexpensive. Related to Bubinga.

BETHABARA (Tabebuis Serratifolia, Vahl.). *Source:* Northern South America. *Color:* olive-brown to blackish heartwood. *Availability:* rare. *Price range:* costly.

BILINGA (Sarcocephalus trillesi, Pierre.). *Source:* West Africa. *Color:* yellow to tan. *Availability:* plentiful as quartered veneer. *Price range:* medium.

BIRCH, DOMESTIC (Betula alleghaniensis, Michx. f.). *Source:* Canada and Northern United States. *Color:* cream to light brown. *Availability:* abundant. *Price range:* medium.

BIRCH, EUROPEAN (Betula alba, Linn.) . *Other names:* Alpine Burl, Finnish Birch, Norway Birch Burl. *Source:* Scandinavia. *Color:* tan to cream. *Availability:* scarce. *Price range:* high.

BLACK BEAN (Castanospermum australe, A. Cunn.) . *Other name:* Beanwood. *Source:* Australia. *Color:* Brown to nearly black. *Availability:* scarce as quartered veneer. *Price range:* costly.

BLACKWOOD, TASMANIAN (Acacia melanoxylon) . *Other names:* Australian Blackwood, Blackwood Acacia. *Source:* Australia and Tasmania. *Color:* lustrous, rich reddish-brown. *Availability:* scarce. *Price range:* high.

BOSSE (Guarea cedrata, Pellegr.). *Other names:* African Cedar, Cedar Mahogany, Cedron, Obobo. *Source:* West Africa. *Color:* pink to light mahogany. *Availability:* scarce as quartered veneer. *Price range:* medium.

BOXWOOD (Buxus sempervirens, Linn.) . *Source:* Europe and Asia. *Color:* yellowish-white. *Availability:* rare. *Price range:* very high.

BUBINGA (Guibourtia demeusii) . *Other names:* African Rosewood, Akume, Kewazinga. *Source:* West Africa. *Color:* red to dark purple. *Availability:* plentiful. *Price range:* costly.

BUTTERNUT (Juglans cinerea) . *Other name:* White Walnut. *Source:* Northern United States and Canada. *Color:* pale brown. *Availability:* rare. *Price range:* medium.

CANALETTA (Cordia gerascanthus, Linn.). *Other names:* Canalete, Cyp, Cypre, Princewood, Solera, Ziricote. *Source:* Northern South America. *Color:* purplish to dark brown. *Availability:* scarce. *Price range:* costly.

CAPOMO (Brosimum alicastrum, Sw.). *Other names:* Breadnut, Capome, Laredo, Lerado Ogechi, Ojoche, Ramon. *Source:* Central America. *Color:* yellow to reddish. *Availability:* plentiful. *Price range:* medium.

CATALPA (Catalpa speciosa, Warder). *Source:* South Central United States. *Color:* brown. *Availability:* scarce. *Price range:* low to medium.

CATIVO (Prioria copaifera, Gris.). *Other names:* Florisa, Tabasara. *Source:* Tropical America, West Indies. *Color:* brown to dingy white. *Availability:* plentiful. *Price range:* low.

CEDAR, AROMATIC RED (Juniperus virginiana, Linn.). *Source:* Eastern United States. *Color:* light red and cream. *Availability:* plentiful. *Price range:* medium.

CEDAR, SPANISH (Cedrela odorata). *Other names:* Brazilian Cedar, Cedrela, Cedro, Honduras Cedar. *Source:* Central and South America. *Color:* light red. *Availability:* plentiful. *Price range:* medium.

CELTIS (Celtis soyauxii, Engl.). *Other names:* Ita, Itako, Ohia. *Source:* West Africa. *Color:* white to pale yellow. *Availability:* scarce. *Price range:* medium.

155

CHEN CHEN (Antiaris africana) . *Other names:* Ako, Quen Quen. *Source:* West Africa. *Color:* white to yellowish-gray. *Availability:* scarce as quartered veneer. *Price range:* low to medium.

CHERRY (Prunus serotina, Ehrh.). *Source:* Northern United States. *Color:* light reddish-brown. *Availability:* plentiful. *Price range:* medium.

CINNAMON (Cinnamomum zeylanicum, Breyn.) . *Source:* Ceylon. *Color:* straw to dark brown. *Availability:* rare. *Price range:* moderate.

COCOBOLO (Dalbergia retusa, Hemsley) . *Other name:* Nambar. *Source:* Central America. *Color:* yellowish-brown. *Availability:* scarce as quartered and sliced veneer. *Price range:* costly.

CYPRESS (Taxodium distichum, Linn.). *Source:* Southeastern United States. *Color:* yellowish-red to salmon. *Availability:* scarce. *Price range:* medium.

EBONY, BLACK (Diospyros tomentosa, Roxb.). *Source:* Northern India. *Color:* black. *Availability:* scarce. *Price range:* costly.

EBONY, MACASSAR (Diospyros melanoxylon, Roxb.) . *Other name:* Marblewood. *Source:* East Indies. *Color:* dark brown to black, streaked with yellow. *Availability:* plentiful as quartered and sliced veneer. *Price range:* costly.

EDINAM (Entandrophagma angolense). *Other names:* Gedu Nohor, Ipaki, Timbi, Jebu Mahogany. *Source:* West Africa. *Color:* reddish-brown. *Availability:* plentiful. *Price range:* medium.

ELM, AMERICAN (Ulmus americana, Linn.). *Source:* Eastern United States. *Color:* light brownish. *Availability:* plentiful. *Price range:* medium.

ELM, BROWN (Ulmus rubra). *Source:* Canada and Middle Western United States. *Color:* dark to reddish-brown. *Availability:* plentiful. *Price range:* medium.

ELM, CARPATHIAN BURL (Ulmus campestris, Linn.). *Source:* France, England, Carpathian Mountains. *Color:* from brick red to light tan. *Availability:* plentiful. *Price range:* very costly.

EMERI (Terminalia ivorensis, A. Chev.). *Other names:* Ireme, Black Afara, Framerie. *Source:* West Africa. *Color:* pale yellow to light brown. *Availability:* plentiful. *Price range:* moderate.

FAUX SATINE (Taxodium distichum, Linn.). *Other name:* Cypress Crotch. *Source:* Southeastern United States. *Color:* yellowish-brown. *Availability:* rare. *Price range:* very costly.

GABOON (Aucoumea klaineana, Pierre). *Other names:* Angouma, Gaboon Wood, Okoume. *Source:* West Africa. *Color:* reddish-brown. *Availability:* plentiful. *Price range:* inexpensive to costly.

GONCALO ALVES (Astronium fraxinifolium, Schott). *Other names:* Gateado, Kingwood, Mura. *Source:* Brazil and Northern South America. *Color:* dark brown to pink. *Availability:* scarce as quartered veneer. *Price range:* costly.

GUAPINO (Hymenaea courbaril, L.). *Other names:* West Indian Locust, South American Locust, Courbaril, Surinam Teak. *Source:* South America. *Color:* dark brown to orange red. *Availability:* rare. *Price range:* inexpensive.

GUM, RED (Liquidambar styraciflua, Linn.). *Other name:* Hazelwood. *Source:* United States. *Availability:* plentiful. *Price range:* medium.

HACKBERRY (Celtis occidentalis, Linn.). *Other name:* Sugarberry. *Source:* Eastern United States. *Color:* yellowish. *Availability:* plentiful. *Price range:* medium.

HAREWOOD (Acer pseudoplatanus, Linn.). *Source:* England. *Color:* white, but usually dyed silver gray. *Availability:* scarce as quartered and sliced veneer. *Price range:* costly.

HICKORY (Carya spp.). *Source:* United States to Mexico. *Color:* white to tan. *Availability:* plentiful. *Price range:* medium.

HOLLY (Ilex opaca, Aiton). *Source:* United States. *Color:* white. *Availability:* scarce as sliced veneer. *Price range:* medium.

IMBUYA (Phoebe porosa, Mez.) . *Other names:* Brazilian Walnut, Determa, Embuia, Imbuia. *Source:* Brazil. *Color:* rich brown. *Availability:* plentiful. *Price range:* medium.

INCA (Not identified). *Source:* Brazil and Argentina. *Color:* reddish-brown. *Availability:* very rare as burl veneer. *Price range:* very costly.

IPE (Tabebuia, spp.). *Source:* South America. *Color:* light to dark yellow. *Availability:* rare. *Price range:* medium to costly.

IROKO (Chlorophora exelsa) . *Other names:* Oroko, Odoum, African Teak. *Source:* West Africa. *Color:* light brown to rich golden brown. *Availability:* rare. *Price range:* low.

KELOBRA (Enterolobium cyclocarpum (Jacq.), Gris.). *Other names:* Guanacaste, Genizero, Jenisero, Parota. *Source:* Mexico and Central America. *Color:* greenish-brown. *Availability:* plentiful. *Price range:* medium.

KINGWOOD (Dalbergia cearensis, Cucke) . *Other name:* Violetwood. *Source:* Northern South America. *Color:* violet to brown, with age. *Availability:* rare. *Price range:* costly.

KOA (Acacia koa, Gray). *Source:* Hawaii. *Color:* golden brown with dark streaks. *Availability:* plentiful. *Price range:* costly.

KOKKO (Albizzia lebbeck). *Other name:* Koko. *Source:* Andaman Islands, Burma, India, and Ceylon. *Color:* brown to gold. *Availability:* rare. *Price range:* costly.

LACEWOOD (Cardwellia sublimis, F. Muell.). *Other names:* Australian Silky Oak, Queensland Silky Oak, Silky Oak, Selano. *Source:* Queensland, Australia. *Color:* light silvery-pink. *Availability:* scarce as quartered veneer. *Price range:* costly.

LAUAN, RED (Shorea negrosensis, Foxw.). *Other name:* Philippine Mahogany. *Source:* Philippine Islands. *Color:* red to brown. *Availability:* abundant. *Price range:* medium.

LAUAN, WHITE (Pentacme contorta, Merr.). *Source:* Philippine Islands. *Color:* pale yellow to reddish-brown. *Availability:* plentiful. *Price range:* inexpensive.

LAUREL, EAST INDIAN (Terminalia tomentosa, W. et A.). *Other names:* East Indian Walnut, Rose Laurel, Camphor Laurel. *Source:* India and Burma. *Color:* brown to gold with black lines. *Availability:* scarce as quartered veneer. *Price range:* very costly.

LIMBA (Terminalia superba, Eng. & Diels.). *Other names:* Korina, Afara, Frake, Offram. *Source:* West Africa. *Color:* pale yellow to light brown. *Availability:* plentiful. *Price range:* medium.

MACAWOOD (Platymiscium, spp.). *Other name:* Brazilian Padauk. *Source:* Northern South America. *Color:* reddish-brown. *Availability:* scarce. *Price range:* expensive.

MADORO (Unidentified). *Other name:* Mindoro. *Source:* Brazil. *Color:* tan to dark brown. *Availability:* rare. *Price range:* moderate to costly.

MADRONE BURL (Arbutus menziesii, Pursh.). *Other names:* Madrona, Madrono. *Source:* Western United States to Mexico. *Color:* reddish-brown. *Availability:* scarce as half-round veneers and burls. *Price range:* costly.

MAGNOLIA (Magnolia grandiflora, Linn.). *Other name:* Cucumber Tree. *Source:* Southern United States. *Color:* greenish-white. *Availability:* plentiful. *Price range:* inexpensive.

MAHOGANY, AFRICAN (Khaya ivorensis, A. Chev.). *Source:* Africa. *Color:* light pink to reddish-brown. *Availability:* abundant. *Price range:* medium to costly.

MAHOGANY, TROPICAL AMERICAN (Swietenia macrophylla, King). *Source:* Mexico, Central and South America. *Color:* rich golden brown. *Availability:* plentiful. *Price range:* medium to costly.

MAI DOU (Pterocarpus pedatus, Pierre). *Other names:* Madou, Mai Padu, False Amboyna Burl. *Source:* Indo-China. *Color:* scarlet and pale straw. *Availability:* very rare. *Price range:* very costly.

MAKORI (Mimusops heckelii, Hutch. & Dalz.). *Other names:* African Cherry, Baku, Cherry Mahogany, Makore. *Source:* West

Africa. *Color:* pinkish-brown to red. *Availability:* plentiful. *Price range:* medium.

MANSONIA (Mansonia altissima, A. Chev.). *Other names:* Aprono, Ofun, Opruno. *Source:* West Africa. *Color:* whitish sapwood to purplish-brown heartwood. *Availability:* plentiful. *Price range:* medium.

MAPLE, HARD (Acer saccharum, Marsh.). *Source:* Northern United States and Canada. *Color:* cream to light reddish-brown. *Availability:* plentiful. *Price range:* medium to costly.

MARNUT (Machaerium, spp.). *Source:* Brazil. *Color:* violet to brown. *Availability:* rare. *Price range:* costly.

MESQUITE BURL (Prosopis juliflora). *Source:* Southwestern United States and Mexico. *Color:* dark reddish-brown. *Availability:* rare. *Price range:* costly.

MOCHA (Andira jamaicensis (W. Wr.), Urb.). *Other names:* Moca, Moca Blanco, Moca Colorado. *Source:* Central America. *Color:* yellow-brown. *Availability:* rare as half-round veneer. *Price range:* high.

MOVINGUI (Distemonanthus benthamianus, Baill.). *Other names:* Anyaran, Ayan, Nigerian Satinwood. *Source:* West Africa. *Color:* light yellow. *Availability:* scarce as quartered and sliced veneers. *Price range:* medium.

MYRTLE (Umbellularia californica, (H. & A.) Nuttall.). *Source:* Southern Oregon and Northern California. *Color:* golden brown and yellowish-green. *Availability:* plentiful as half-round veneers. *Price range:* high.

NARRA (Pterocarpus indicus, Willd.). *Other names:* Angsena, Sena. *Source:* Borneo, Dutch East Indies, and the Philippine Islands. *Color:* rose to deep red or golden yellow-brown. *Availability:* plentiful. *Price range:* costly.

NEW GUINEA WOOD (Dracontomelum magiferum, Blume). *Other names:* Guinea Wood, Guinea Walnut. *Source:* New Guinea and the Philippine Islands. *Color:* brown and yellow stripes. *Availability:* plentiful. *Price range:* moderate to costly.

OAK, AMERICAN (Quercus alba, Linn.). *Source:* Eastern United States. *Color:* white to pinkish. *Availability:* plentiful. *Price range:* medium.

OAK, ENGLISH BROWN (Quercus robur, L.Q.). *Source:* England. *Color:* light tan to deep brown. *Availability:* becoming scarce. *Price range:* costly.

OPEPE (Sarcocephalus diderrichii, De Wild.). *Other name:* Abiache. *Source:* Africa. *Color:* grayish-white to orange. *Availability:* plentiful. *Price range:* inexpensive.

ORIENTALWOOD (Endiandra palmerstoni, C.T. White). *Other names:* Australian Laurel, Australian Walnut, Oriental Walnut.

Source: Australia. *Color:* pinkish-gray to brown. *Availability:* plentiful. *Price range:* costly.

ORO (Pahudia rhomboidea (bleo.), Prain.). *Other name.* Tindalo. *Source:* Philippine Islands. *Color:* pale orange to deep wine and black. *Availability:* rare. *Price range:* high.

PADAUK, AFRICAN (Pterocarpus Soyauxii, Taub.). *Other names:* Corail, Padouk. *Source:* African West Coast. *Color:* golden red. *Availability:* scarce as quartered and sliced veneers. *Price range:* costly.

PADAUK, ANDAMAN (Pterocarpus dalbergioides, Roxb.). *Other name:* Vermilion. *Source:* Andaman Islands. *Color:* golden brown to violet red. *Availability:* rare as quartered and sliced veneers. *Price range:* very costly.

PADAUK, ANGOLA (Pterocarpus angolensis). *Other name:* Muninga. *Source:* East Africa. *Color:* golden to dark brown streaked with yellow. *Availability:* plentiful. *Price range:* moderate.

PADAUK, BURMESE (Pterocarpus macrocarpus, Kurz.). *Other name:* Vermilion. *Source:* Burma. *Color:* yellow and reddish-brown. *Availability:* scarce. *Price range:* costly.

PALDAO (Dracontomelum dao, Merr. & Rolfe.). *Other name:* Dao. *Source:* Philippine Islands. *Color:* gray to reddish-brown with dark stripes. *Availability:* plentiful. *Price range:* medium.

PEARWOOD (Pyrus communis, Linn.). *Source:* Europe and the United States. *Color:* rosy-cream. *Availability:* scarce as sliced veneer. *Price range:* costly.

PECAN (Carya illinoensis, K. Koch). *Source:* Southern United States. *Color:* reddish-brown to creamy-white. *Availability:* plentiful. *Price range:* medium.

PENDA (Xanthostemon oppositifolius). *Source:* Australia. *Color:* grayish-brown with chocolate brown stripes. *Availability:* uncommon. *Price range:* inexpensive.

PEROBA, WHITE (Paratecoma peroba, Kuhl.). *Other names:* Peroba Amarella, Peroba Branca. *Source:* Brazil. *Color:* olive to golden. *Availability:* scarce as quartered and sliced veneers. *Price range:* costly.

PEROBA, RED (Aspidosperma polyneuron, Muell. Arg.). *Other names:* Peroba Rosa, Palo Rosa. *Source:* Brazil. *Color:* pale rose with dark streaks. *Availability:* plentiful. *Price range:* medium.

PINE, KNOTTY (Pinus monticola, D. Don.). *Source:* Northwestern United States. *Color:* light brown or red. *Availability:* plentiful. *Price range:* medium.

PRIMAVERA (Cybistax donnell-smithii, Rose). *Other names:* Durango, Palo Blanco, San Juan, White Mahogany. *Source:* Mexico to Central America. *Color:* yellow-white to yellow-brown. *Availability:* plentiful. *Price range:* costly.

REDWOOD BURL (Sequoia sempervirens (Lam.), Endlicher). *Source:* California. *Color:* pink to deep red. *Availability:* scarce as half-round veneer. *Price range:* costly.

ROSEWOOD, BRAZILIAN (Dalbergia nigra, Fr. Allem.). *Other names:* Bahia Rosewood, Jacaranda, Rio Rosewood. *Source:* Brazil. *Color:* Chocolate to violet. *Availability:* abundant. *Price range:* costly.

ROSEWOOD, EAST INDIAN (Dalbergia latifolia, Roxb.). *Other names:* Bombay Rosewood, Blackwood, Malobar. *Source:* Southern India and Ceylon. *Color:* dark purple to ebony with streaks of black. *Availability:* plentiful. *Price range:* costly.

ROSEWOOD, HONDURAS (Dalbergia stevensonii, Standl.). *Source:* Central America. *Color:* pinkish-brown to purplish with dark streaks. *Availability:* scarce as quartered and sliced veneers. *Price range:* costly.

ROSEWOOD, MADAGASCAR (Dalbergia greveana, Baill.). *Other names:* Madagascar Palisander, French Rosewood, Faux Rose, Palisander. *Source:* Madagascar. *Color:* dark to light rose-pink with pronounced dark streaks. *Availability:* scarce. *Price range:* costly.

SABICU (Lysiloma sabicu, Bth.). *Source:* Central America. *Color:* pink to dark red. *Availability:* scarce. *Price range:* inexpensive.

SAPELE (Entandrophragma cylindricum, Sprague). *Other names:*

Aboudikrou, Sipo, Tiama. *Source:* West Africa. *Color:* dark red-brown. *Availability:* plentiful. *Price range:* medium.

SATINWOOD, CEYLON (Chloroxylon swietenia, D.C.). *Other name:* East Indian Satinwood. *Source:* Ceylon and Southern India. *Color:* pale gold. *Availability:* plentiful. *Price range:* costly.

SATINWOOD, WEST INDIAN (Zanthoxylum flavum, Vahl.). *Other name:* San Domingan Satinwood. *Source:* Puerto Rico and British Honduras. *Color:* golden yellow. *Availability:* scarce as sliced veneer. *Price range:* costly.

SANTA VERA (Eucalyptus, spp.). *Source:* Australia. *Color:* pinkish-brown. *Availability:* plentiful. *Price range:* medium.

SISSO (Dalbergia sissoo, Roxb.). *Source:* India. *Color:* rich warm brown. *Availability:* rare. *Price range:* costly.

SNAKEWOOD (Piratinera guianensis, Aubl.). *Other names:* Letterwood, Leopard Wood. *Source:* British Guiana and British Honduras. *Color:* warm reddish-brown with black streaks. *Availability:* rare. *Price range:* very costly.

SONORA (Shorea philippinensis). *Other names:* Manggasinoro, Sinora. *Source:* Philippine Islands. *Color:* yellow-white to pale brown. *Availability:* plentiful. *Price range:* medium.

SUCUPIRA (Bowdichia, spp.). *Other names:* Acapa, Amoteak. *Source:* Brazil and Venezuela. *Color:* deep chocolate brown. *Availability:* rare. *Price range:* inexpensive.

SYCAMORE (Platanus occidentalis, Linn.). *Source:* United States. *Color:* pale reddish-brown. *Availability:* plentiful. *Price range:* inexpensive.

TEAK (Tectona grandis, L.F.). *Source:* Burma, Java, India, and Indo-China. *Color:* tawny yellow to dark brown. *Availability:* plentiful. *Price range:* costly.

TANGUILE (Shorea polysperma, Merr.). *Other names:* Tangile, Bataan. *Source:* Philippine Islands. *Color:* pale to dark reddish-brown. *Availability:* plentiful. *Price range:* medium.

TEPESUCHIL (Cordia alliodora (R. & P.), Chem.). *Source:* Tropical America. *Color:* greenish-gray. *Availability:* rare. *Price range:* costly.

THUYA BURL (Tetraclinis articulata, Masters). *Source:* The Atlas Mountains of Algeria. *Color:* yellowish-brown to red. *Availability:* scarce as half-round veneer. *Price range:* costly to very costly.

TIGERWOOD (Lovoa trichilioides, Pierre). *Other names:* Congowood, Benin, African Walnut, Benin Walnut, Nigerian Golden Walnut. *Source:* West Africa. *Color:* gray-brown to gold with black streaks. *Availability:* plentiful. *Price range:* medium.

TOLA (Oxystigma oxyphyllum, Harms.). *Other names:* White Tola, Agba. *Source:* West Africa. *Color:* medium brown to faint purple. *Availability:* scarce. *Price range:* moderate.

TULIPWOOD (Dalbergia frutescens *var.* tomentosa). *Other names:* Brazilian Pinkwood, Bois De Rose. *Source:* Northeastern Brazil. *Color:* red and yellow streaks. *Availability:* scarce as sliced veneer. *Price range:* costly.

WALNUT, AMERICAN BLACK (Juglans nigra, Linn.). *Source:* United States. *Color:* light gray-brown to dark purplish-brown. *Availability:* abundant. *Price range:* medium to costly.

WALNUT, FRENCH (Juglans regia, Linn.). *Source:* France and Europe. *Color:* lighter than American Walnut, with prominent light stripes at times. *Availability:* scarce. *Price range:* expensive.

WENGE (Milletia laurentii). *Other name:* Dikela. *Source:* The Congo. *Color:* dark brown with fine black lines. *Availability:* plentiful. *Price range:* costly.

YELLOWPOPLAR (Liriodendron tulipifera, Linn.). *Other names:* Tuliptree, Whitewood. *Source:* United States. *Color:* canary yellow to greenish. *Availability:* abundant. *Price range:* inexpensive.

YEW, AMERICAN (Taxus brevifolia). *Source:* Pacific coast and Canada. *Color:* reddish-brown. *Availability:* rare. *Price range:* costly.

YEW, ENGLISH (Taxus baccata, Linn.). *Source:* England. *Color:* pale red. *Availability:* rare. *Price range:* very costly.

YUBA (Eucalyptus obliqua, L'Herit.). *Other name:* Tasmanian Oak. *Source:* Tasmania and Australia. *Color:* light tan to golden brown. *Availability:* rare. *Price range:* expensive.

ZAPOTA (Achras zapota, L.). *Other names:* Sapodilla, Naseberry, Chico Zapote, Zapotilla. *Source:* Mexico and Central America. *Color:* deep rich red to plum. *Availability:* rare. *Price range:* costly.

ZEBRAWOOD (Microberlinia brazzavillanensis). *Other names:* Zebrano, Zingana. *Source:* West Africa. *Color:* straw and dark brown stripes. *Availability:* plentiful. *Price range:* costly.

INDEX

INDEX

173

A CATALOG OF SELECTED
DOVER BOOKS
IN ALL FIELDS OF INTEREST

A CATALOG OF SELECTED
DOVER BOOKS
IN ALL FIELDS OF INTEREST

DRAWINGS OF REMBRANDT, edited by Seymour Slive. Updated Lippmann, Hofstede de Groot edition, with definitive scholarly apparatus. All portraits, biblical sketches, landscapes, nudes. Oriental figures, classical studies, together with selection of work by followers. 550 illustrations. Total of 630pp. 9⅛ × 12¼.
21485-0, 21486-9 Pa., Two-vol. set $29.90

GHOST AND HORROR STORIES OF AMBROSE BIERCE, Ambrose Bierce. 24 tales vividly imagined, strangely prophetic, and decades ahead of their time in technical skill: "The Damned Thing," "An Inhabitant of Carcosa," "The Eyes of the Panther," "Moxon's Master," and 20 more. 199pp. 5⅜ × 8½. 20767-6 Pa. $4.95

ETHICAL WRITINGS OF MAIMONIDES, Maimonides. Most significant ethical works of great medieval sage, newly translated for utmost precision, readability. Laws Concerning Character Traits, Eight Chapters, more. 192pp. 5⅜ × 8½.
24522-5 Pa. $4.50

THE EXPLORATION OF THE COLORADO RIVER AND ITS CANYONS, J. W. Powell. Full text of Powell's 1,000-mile expedition down the fabled Colorado in 1869. Superb account of terrain, geology, vegetation, Indians, famine, mutiny, treacherous rapids, mighty canyons, during exploration of last unknown part of continental U.S. 400pp. 5⅜ × 8½. 20094-9 Pa. $7.95

HISTORY OF PHILOSOPHY, Julián Marías. Clearest one-volume history on the market. Every major philosopher and dozens of others, to Existentialism and later. 505pp. 5⅜ × 8½. 21739-6 Pa. $9.95

ALL ABOUT LIGHTNING, Martin A. Uman. Highly readable nontechnical survey of nature and causes of lightning, thunderstorms, ball lightning, St. Elmo's Fire, much more. Illustrated. 192pp. 5⅜ × 8½. 25237-X Pa. $5.95

SAILING ALONE AROUND THE WORLD, Captain Joshua Slocum. First man to sail around the world, alone, in small boat. One of great feats of seamanship told in delightful manner. 67 illustrations. 294pp. 5⅜ × 8½. 20326-3 Pa. $4.95

LETTERS AND NOTES ON THE MANNERS, CUSTOMS AND CONDITIONS OF THE NORTH AMERICAN INDIANS, George Catlin. Classic account of life among Plains Indians: ceremonies, hunt, warfare, etc. 312 plates. 572pp. of text. 6⅛ × 9¼. 22118-0, 22119-9, Pa., Two-vol. set $17.90

ALASKA: The Harriman Expedition, 1899, John Burroughs, John Muir, et al. Informative, engrossing accounts of two-month, 9,000-mile expedition. Native peoples, wildlife, forests, geography, salmon industry, glaciers, more. Profusely illustrated. 240 black-and-white line drawings. 124 black-and-white photographs. 3 maps. Index. 576pp. 5⅜ × 8½. 25109-8 Pa. $11.95

THE BOOK OF BEASTS: Being a Translation from a Latin Bestiary of the Twelfth Century, T. H. White. Wonderful catalog of real and fanciful beasts: manticore, griffin, phoenix, amphivius, jaculus, many more. White's witty erudite commentary on scientific, historical aspects enhances fascinating glimpse of medieval mind. Illustrated. 296pp. 5⅜ × 8¼. (Available in U.S. only) 24609-4 Pa. $6.95

FRANK LLOYD WRIGHT: Architecture and Nature with 160 Illustrations, Donald Hoffmann. Profusely illustrated study of influence of nature—especially prairie—on Wright's designs for Fallingwater, Robie House, Guggenheim Museum, other masterpieces. 96pp. 9¼ × 10¾. 25098-9 Pa. $8.95

FRANK LLOYD WRIGHT'S FALLINGWATER, Donald Hoffmann. Wright's famous waterfall house: planning and construction of organic idea. History of site, owners, Wright's personal involvement. Photographs of various stages of building. Preface by Edgar Kaufmann, Jr. 100 illustrations. 112pp. 9¼ × 10.
23671-4 Pa. $8.95

YEARS WITH FRANK LLOYD WRIGHT: Apprentice to Genius, Edgar Tafel. Insightful memoir by a former apprentice presents a revealing portrait of Wright the man, the inspired teacher, the greatest American architect. 372 black-and-white illustrations. Preface. Index. vi + 228pp. 8¼ × 11. 24801-1 Pa. $10.95

THE STORY OF KING ARTHUR AND HIS KNIGHTS, Howard Pyle. Enchanting version of King Arthur fable has delighted generations with imaginative narratives of exciting adventures and unforgettable illustrations by the author. 41 illustrations. xviii + 313pp. 6⅛ × 9¼. 21445-1 Pa. $6.95

THE GODS OF THE EGYPTIANS, E. A. Wallis Budge. Thorough coverage of numerous gods of ancient Egypt by foremost Egyptologist. Information on evolution of cults, rites and gods; the cult of Osiris; the Book of the Dead and its rites; the sacred animals and birds; Heaven and Hell; and more. 956pp. 6⅛ × 9¼.
22055-9, 22056-7 Pa., Two-vol. set $21.90

A THEOLOGICO-POLITICAL TREATISE, Benedict Spinoza. Also contains unfinished *Political Treatise*. Great classic on religious liberty, theory of government on common consent. R. Elwes translation. Total of 421pp. 5⅜ × 8½.
20249-6 Pa. $7.95

INCIDENTS OF TRAVEL IN CENTRAL AMERICA, CHIAPAS, AND YUCATAN, John L. Stephens. Almost single-handed discovery of Maya culture; exploration of ruined cities, monuments, temples; customs of Indians. 115 drawings. 892pp. 5⅜ × 8½. 22404-X, 22405-8 Pa., Two-vol. set $17.90

LOS CAPRICHOS, Francisco Goya. 80 plates of wild, grotesque monsters and caricatures. Prado manuscript included. 183pp. 6⅝ × 9⅜. 22384-1 Pa. $5.95

AUTOBIOGRAPHY: The Story of My Experiments with Truth, Mohandas K. Gandhi. Not hagiography, but Gandhi in his own words. Boyhood, legal studies, purification, the growth of the Satyagraha (nonviolent protest) movement. Critical, inspiring work of the man who freed India. 480pp. 5⅜ × 8½. (Available in U.S. only)
24593-4 Pa. $6.95

ILLUSTRATED DICTIONARY OF HISTORIC ARCHITECTURE, edited by Cyril M. Harris. Extraordinary compendium of clear, concise definitions for over 5,000 important architectural terms complemented by over 2,000 line drawings. Covers full spectrum of architecture from ancient ruins to 20th-century Modernism. Preface. 592pp. 7½ × 9⅝. 24444-X Pa. $15.95

THE NIGHT BEFORE CHRISTMAS, Clement C. Moore. Full text, and woodcuts from original 1848 book. Also critical, historical material. 19 illustrations. 40pp. 4⅝ × 6. 22797-9 Pa. $2.50

THE LESSON OF JAPANESE ARCHITECTURE: 165 Photographs, Jiro Harada. Memorable gallery of 165 photographs taken in the 1930s of exquisite Japanese homes of the well-to-do and historic buildings. 13 line diagrams. 192pp. 8⅜ × 11¼. 24778-3 Pa. $10.95

THE AUTOBIOGRAPHY OF CHARLES DARWIN AND SELECTED LETTERS, edited by Francis Darwin. The fascinating life of eccentric genius composed of an intimate memoir by Darwin (intended for his children); commentary by his son, Francis; hundreds of fragments from notebooks, journals, papers; and letters to and from Lyell, Hooker, Huxley, Wallace and Henslow. xi + 365pp. 5⅜ × 8. 20479-0 Pa. $6.95

WONDERS OF THE SKY: Observing Rainbows, Comets, Eclipses, the Stars and Other Phenomena, Fred Schaaf. Charming, easy-to-read poetic guide to all manner of celestial events visible to the naked eye. Mock suns, glories, Belt of Venus, more. Illustrated. 299pp. 5¼ × 8¼. 24402-4 Pa. $8.95

BURNHAM'S CELESTIAL HANDBOOK, Robert Burnham, Jr. Thorough guide to the stars beyond our solar system. Exhaustive treatment. Alphabetical by constellation: Andromeda to Cetus in Vol. 1; Chamaeleon to Orion in Vol. 2; and Pavo to Vulpecula in Vol. 3. Hundreds of illustrations. Index in Vol. 3. 2,000pp. 6⅛ × 9¼. 23567-X, 23568-8, 23673-0 Pa., Three-vol. set $41.85

STAR NAMES: Their Lore and Meaning, Richard Hinckley Allen. Fascinating history of names various cultures have given to constellations and literary and folkloristic uses that have been made of stars. Indexes to subjects. Arabic and Greek names. Biblical references. Bibliography. 563pp. 5⅜ × 8½. 21079-0 Pa. $8.95

THIRTY YEARS THAT SHOOK PHYSICS: The Story of Quantum Theory, George Gamow. Lucid, accessible introduction to influential theory of energy and matter. Careful explanations of Dirac's anti-particles, Bohr's model of the atom, much more. 12 plates. Numerous drawings. 240pp. 5⅜ × 8½. 24895-X Pa. $6.95

CHINESE DOMESTIC FURNITURE IN PHOTOGRAPHS AND MEASURED DRAWINGS, Gustav Ecke. A rare volume, now affordably priced for antique collectors, furniture buffs and art historians. Detailed review of styles ranging from early Shang to late Ming. Unabridged republication. 161 black-and-white drawings, photos. Total of 224pp. 8⅜ × 11¼. (Available in U.S. only) 25171-3 Pa. $14.95

VINCENT VAN GOGH: A Biography, Julius Meier-Graefe. Dynamic, penetrating study of artist's life, relationship with brother, Theo, painting techniques, travels, more. Readable, engrossing. 160pp. 5⅜ × 8½. (Available in U.S. only) 25253-1 Pa. $4.95

HOW TO WRITE, Gertrude Stein. Gertrude Stein claimed anyone could understand her unconventional writing—here are clues to help. Fascinating improvisations, language experiments, explanations illuminate Stein's craft and the art of writing. Total of 414pp. 4⅝ × 6⅜. 23144-5 Pa. $6.95

ADVENTURES AT SEA IN THE GREAT AGE OF SAIL: Five Firsthand Narratives, edited by Elliot Snow. Rare true accounts of exploration, whaling, shipwreck, fierce natives, trade, shipboard life, more. 33 illustrations. Introduction. 353pp. 5⅜ × 8½. 25177-2 Pa. $9.95

THE HERBAL OR GENERAL HISTORY OF PLANTS, John Gerard. Classic descriptions of about 2,850 plants—with over 2,700 illustrations—includes Latin and English names, physical descriptions, varieties, time and place of growth, more. 2,706 illustrations. xlv + 1,678pp. 8½ × 12¼. 23147-X Cloth. $75.00

DOROTHY AND THE WIZARD IN OZ, L. Frank Baum. Dorothy and the Wizard visit the center of the Earth, where people are vegetables, glass houses grow and Oz characters reappear. Classic sequel to *Wizard of Oz*. 256pp. 5⅜ × 8. 24714-7 Pa. $5.95

SONGS OF EXPERIENCE: Facsimile Reproduction with 26 Plates in Full Color, William Blake. This facsimile of Blake's original "Illuminated Book" reproduces 26 full-color plates from a rare 1826 edition. Includes "The Tyger," "London," "Holy Thursday," and other immortal poems. 26 color plates. Printed text of poems. 48pp. 5¼ × 7. 24636-1 Pa. $3.95

SONGS OF INNOCENCE, William Blake. The first and most popular of Blake's famous "Illuminated Books," in a facsimile edition reproducing all 31 brightly colored plates. Additional printed text of each poem. 64pp. 5¼ × 7. 22764-2 Pa. $3.95

PRECIOUS STONES, Max Bauer. Classic, thorough study of diamonds, rubies, emeralds, garnets, etc.: physical character, occurrence, properties, use, similar topics. 20 plates, 8 in color. 94 figures. 659pp. 6⅛ × 9¼. 21910-0, 21911-9 Pa., Two-vol. set $15.90

ENCYCLOPEDIA OF VICTORIAN NEEDLEWORK, S. F. A. Caulfeild and Blanche Saward. Full, precise descriptions of stitches, techniques for dozens of needlecrafts—most exhaustive reference of its kind. Over 800 figures. Total of 679pp. 8⅛ × 11. 22800-2, 22801-0 Pa., Two-vol. set $23.90

THE MARVELOUS LAND OF OZ, L. Frank Baum. Second Oz book, the Scarecrow and Tin Woodman are back with hero named Tip, Oz magic. 136 illustrations. 287pp. 5⅜ × 8½. 20692-0 Pa. $5.95

WILD FOWL DECOYS, Joel Barber. Basic book on the subject, by foremost authority and collector. Reveals history of decoy making and rigging, place in American culture, different kinds of decoys, how to make them, and how to use them. 140 plates. 156pp. 7⅞ × 10¾. 20011-6 Pa. $8.95

HISTORY OF LACE, Mrs. Bury Palliser. Definitive, profusely illustrated chronicle of lace from earliest times to late 19th century. Laces of Italy, Greece, England, France, Belgium, etc. Landmark of needlework scholarship. 266 illustrations. 672pp. 6⅛ × 9¼. 24742-2 Pa. $16.95

CATALOG OF DOVER BOOKS

ILLUSTRATED GUIDE TO SHAKER FURNITURE, Robert Meader. All furniture and appurtenances, with much on unknown local styles. 235 photos. 146pp. 9 × 12. 22819-3 Pa. $8.95

WHALE SHIPS AND WHALING: A Pictorial Survey, George Francis Dow. Over 200 vintage engravings, drawings, photographs of barks, brigs, cutters, other vessels. Also harpoons, lances, whaling guns, many other artifacts. Comprehensive text by foremost authority. 207 black-and-white illustrations. 288pp. 6 × 9. 24808-9 Pa. $9.95

THE BERTRAMS, Anthony Trollope. Powerful portrayal of blind self-will and thwarted ambition includes one of Trollope's most heartrending love stories. 497pp. 5⅜ × 8½. 25119-5 Pa. $9.95

ADVENTURES WITH A HAND LENS, Richard Headstrom. Clearly written guide to observing and studying flowers and grasses, fish scales, moth and insect wings, egg cases, buds, feathers, seeds, leaf scars, moss, molds, ferns, common crystals, etc.—all with an ordinary, inexpensive magnifying glass. 209 exact line drawings aid in your discoveries. 220pp. 5⅜ × 8½. 23330-8 Pa. $5.95

RODIN ON ART AND ARTISTS, Auguste Rodin. Great sculptor's candid, wide-ranging comments on meaning of art; great artists; relation of sculpture to poetry, painting, music; philosophy of life, more. 76 superb black-and-white illustrations of Rodin's sculpture, drawings and prints. 119pp. 8⅜ × 11¼. 24487-3 Pa. $7.95

FIFTY CLASSIC FRENCH FILMS, 1912–1982: A Pictorial Record, Anthony Slide. Memorable stills from Grand Illusion, Beauty and the Beast, Hiroshima, Mon Amour, many more. Credits, plot synopses, reviews, etc. 160pp. 8¼ × 11. 25256-6 Pa. $11.95

THE PRINCIPLES OF PSYCHOLOGY, William James. Famous long course complete, unabridged. Stream of thought, time perception, memory, experimental methods; great work decades ahead of its time. 94 figures. 1,391pp. 5⅜ × 8½. 20381-6, 20382-4 Pa., Two-vol. set $25.90

BODIES IN A BOOKSHOP, R. T. Campbell. Challenging mystery of blackmail and murder with ingenious plot and superbly drawn characters. In the best tradition of British suspense fiction. 192pp. 5⅜ × 8½. 24720-1 Pa. $4.95

CALLAS: Portrait of a Prima Donna, George Jellinek. Renowned commentator on the musical scene chronicles incredible career and life of the most controversial, fascinating, influential operatic personality of our time. 64 black-and-white photographs. 416pp. 5⅜ × 8¼. 25047-4 Pa. $8.95

GEOMETRY, RELATIVITY AND THE FOURTH DIMENSION, Rudolph Rucker. Exposition of fourth dimension, concepts of relativity as Flatland characters continue adventures. Popular, easily followed yet accurate, profound. 141 illustrations. 133pp. 5⅜ × 8½. 23400-2 Pa. $4.95

HOUSEHOLD STORIES BY THE BROTHERS GRIMM, with pictures by Walter Crane. 53 classic stories—Rumpelstiltskin, Rapunzel, Hansel and Gretel, the Fisherman and his Wife, Snow White, Tom Thumb, Sleeping Beauty, Cinderella, and so much more—lavishly illustrated with original 19th-century drawings. 114 illustrations. x + 269pp. 5⅜ × 8½. 21080-4 Pa. $4.95

SUNDIALS, Albert Waugh. Far and away the best, most thorough coverage of ideas, mathematics concerned, types, construction, adjusting anywhere. Over 100 illustrations. 230pp. 5⅜ × 8½. 22947-5 Pa. $5.95

PICTURE HISTORY OF THE NORMANDIE: With 190 Illustrations, Frank O. Braynard. Full story of legendary French ocean liner: Art Deco interiors, design innovations, furnishings, celebrities, maiden voyage, tragic fire, much more. Extensive text. 144pp. 8⅞ × 11¾. 25257-4 Pa. $10.95

THE FIRST AMERICAN COOKBOOK: A Facsimile of "American Cookery," 1796, Amelia Simmons. Facsimile of the first American-written cookbook published in the United States contains authentic recipes for colonial favorites—pumpkin pudding, winter squash pudding, spruce beer, Indian slapjacks, and more. Introductory Essay and Glossary of colonial cooking terms. 80pp. 5⅜ × 8½. 24710-4 Pa. $3.50

101 PUZZLES IN THOUGHT AND LOGIC, C. R. Wylie, Jr. Solve murders and robberies, find out which fishermen are liars, how a blind man could possibly identify a color—purely by your own reasoning! 107pp. 5⅜ × 8½. 20367-0 Pa. $2.95

ANCIENT EGYPTIAN MYTHS AND LEGENDS, Lewis Spence. Examines animism, totemism, fetishism, creation myths, deities, alchemy, art and magic, other topics. Over 50 illustrations. 432pp. 5⅜ × 8½. 26525-0 Pa. $8.95

ANTHROPOLOGY AND MODERN LIFE, Franz Boas. Great anthropologist's classic treatise on race and culture. Introduction by Ruth Bunzel. Only inexpensive paperback edition. 255pp. 5⅜ × 8½. 25245-0 Pa. $6.95

THE TALE OF PETER RABBIT, Beatrix Potter. The inimitable Peter's terrifying adventure in Mr. McGregor's garden, with all 27 wonderful, full-color Potter illustrations. 55pp. 4¼ × 5½. (Available in U.S. only) 22827-4 Pa. $1.75

THREE PROPHETIC SCIENCE FICTION NOVELS, H. G. Wells. *When the Sleeper Wakes, A Story of the Days to Come* and *The Time Machine* (full version). 335pp. 5⅜ × 8½. (Available in U.S. only) 20605-X Pa. $8.95

APICIUS COOKERY AND DINING IN IMPERIAL ROME, edited and translated by Joseph Dommers Vehling. Oldest known cookbook in existence offers readers a clear picture of what foods Romans ate, how they prepared them, etc. 49 illustrations. 301pp. 6⅛ × 9¼. 23563-7 Pa. $7.95

SHAKESPEARE LEXICON AND QUOTATION DICTIONARY, Alexander Schmidt. Full definitions, locations, shades of meaning of every word in plays and poems. More than 50,000 exact quotations. 1,485pp. 6½ × 9¼. 22726-X, 22727-8 Pa., Two-vol. set $31.90

THE WORLD'S GREAT SPEECHES, edited by Lewis Copeland and Lawrence W. Lamm. Vast collection of 278 speeches from Greeks to 1970. Powerful and effective models; unique look at history. 842pp. 5⅜ × 8½. 20468-5 Pa. $12.95

THE BLUE FAIRY BOOK, Andrew Lang. The first, most famous collection, with many familiar tales: Little Red Riding Hood, Aladdin and the Wonderful Lamp, Puss in Boots, Sleeping Beauty, Hansel and Gretel, Rumpelstiltskin; 37 in all. 138 illustrations. 390pp. 5⅜ × 8½. 21437-0 Pa. $6.95

THE STORY OF THE CHAMPIONS OF THE ROUND TABLE, Howard Pyle. Sir Launcelot, Sir Tristram and Sir Percival in spirited adventures of love and triumph retold in Pyle's inimitable style. 50 drawings, 31 full-page. xviii + 329pp. 6½ × 9¼. 21883-X Pa. $7.95

THE MYTHS OF THE NORTH AMERICAN INDIANS, Lewis Spence. Myths and legends of the Algonquins, Iroquois, Pawnees and Sioux with comprehensive historical and ethnological commentary. 36 illustrations. 5⅜ × 8½. 25967-6 Pa. $8.95

GREAT DINOSAUR HUNTERS AND THEIR DISCOVERIES, Edwin H. Colbert. Fascinating, lavishly illustrated chronicle of dinosaur research, 1820s to 1960. Achievements of Cope, Marsh, Brown, Buckland, Mantell, Huxley, many others. 384pp. 5¼ × 8¼. 24701-5 Pa. $7.95

THE TASTEMAKERS, Russell Lynes. Informal, illustrated social history of American taste 1850s–1950s. First popularized categories Highbrow, Lowbrow, Middlebrow. 129 illustrations. New (1979) afterword. 384pp. 6 × 9. 23993-4 Pa. $8.95

DOUBLE CROSS PURPOSES, Ronald A. Knox. A treasure hunt in the Scottish Highlands, an old map, unidentified corpse, surprise discoveries keep reader guessing in this cleverly intricate tale of financial skullduggery. 2 black-and-white maps. 320pp. 5⅜ × 8½. (Available in U.S. only) 25032-6 Pa. $6.95

AUTHENTIC VICTORIAN DECORATION AND ORNAMENTATION IN FULL COLOR: 46 Plates from "Studies in Design," Christopher Dresser. Superb full-color lithographs reproduced from rare original portfolio of a major Victorian designer. 48pp. 9¼ × 12¼. 25083-0 Pa. $7.95

PRIMITIVE ART, Franz Boas. Remains the best text ever prepared on subject, thoroughly discussing Indian, African, Asian, Australian, and, especially, Northern American primitive art. Over 950 illustrations show ceramics, masks, totem poles, weapons, textiles, paintings, much more. 376pp. 5⅜ × 8. 20025-6 Pa. $7.95

SIDELIGHTS ON RELATIVITY, Albert Einstein. Unabridged republication of two lectures delivered by the great physicist in 1920–21. *Ether and Relativity* and *Geometry and Experience*. Elegant ideas in nonmathematical form, accessible to intelligent layman. vi + 56pp. 5⅜ × 8½. 24511-X Pa. $3.95

THE WIT AND HUMOR OF OSCAR WILDE, edited by Alvin Redman. More than 1,000 ripostes, paradoxes, wisecracks: Work is the curse of the drinking classes, I can resist everything except temptation, etc. 258pp. 5⅜ × 8½. 20602-5 Pa. $4.95

ADVENTURES WITH A MICROSCOPE, Richard Headstrom. 59 adventures with clothing fibers, protozoa, ferns and lichens, roots and leaves, much more. 142 illustrations. 232pp. 5⅜ × 8½. 23471-1 Pa. $3.95

CATALOG OF DOVER BOOKS

PLANTS OF THE BIBLE, Harold N. Moldenke and Alma L. Moldenke. Standard reference to all 230 plants mentioned in Scriptures. Latin name, biblical reference, uses, modern identity, much more. Unsurpassed encyclopedic resource for scholars, botanists, nature lovers, students of Bible. Bibliography. Indexes. 123 black-and-white illustrations. 384pp. 6 × 9. 25069-5 Pa. $8.95

FAMOUS AMERICAN WOMEN: A Biographical Dictionary from Colonial Times to the Present, Robert McHenry, ed. From Pocahontas to Rosa Parks, 1,035 distinguished American women documented in separate biographical entries. Accurate, up-to-date data, numerous categories, spans 400 years. Indices. 493pp. 6½ × 9¼. 24523-3 Pa. $10.95

THE FABULOUS INTERIORS OF THE GREAT OCEAN LINERS IN HISTORIC PHOTOGRAPHS, William H. Miller, Jr. Some 200 superb photographs capture exquisite interiors of world's great "floating palaces"—1890s to 1980s: Titanic, Ile de France, Queen Elizabeth, United States, Europa, more. Approx. 200 black-and-white photographs. Captions. Text. Introduction. 160pp. 8⅜ × 11¾. 24756-2 Pa. $9.95

THE GREAT LUXURY LINERS, 1927–1954: A Photographic Record, William H. Miller, Jr. Nostalgic tribute to heyday of ocean liners. 186 photos of Ile de France, Normandie, Leviathan, Queen Elizabeth, United States, many others. Interior and exterior views. Introduction. Captions. 160pp. 9 × 12. 24056-8 Pa. $10.95

A NATURAL HISTORY OF THE DUCKS, John Charles Phillips. Great landmark of ornithology offers complete detailed coverage of nearly 200 species and subspecies of ducks: gadwall, sheldrake, merganser, pintail, many more. 74 full-color plates, 102 black-and-white. Bibliography. Total of 1,920pp. 8⅜ × 11¼. 25141-1, 25142-X Cloth., Two-vol. set $100.00

THE SEAWEED HANDBOOK: An Illustrated Guide to Seaweeds from North Carolina to Canada, Thomas F. Lee. Concise reference covers 78 species. Scientific and common names, habitat, distribution, more. Finding keys for easy identification. 224pp. 5⅜ × 8½. 25215-9 Pa. $6.95

THE TEN BOOKS OF ARCHITECTURE: The 1755 Leoni Edition, Leon Battista Alberti. Rare classic helped introduce the glories of ancient architecture to the Renaissance. 68 black-and-white plates. 336pp. 8⅜ × 11¼. 25239-6 Pa. $14.95

MISS MACKENZIE, Anthony Trollope. Minor masterpieces by Victorian master unmasks many truths about life in 19th-century England. First inexpensive edition in years. 392pp. 5⅜ × 8½. 25201-9 Pa. $8.95

THE RIME OF THE ANCIENT MARINER, Gustave Doré, Samuel Taylor Coleridge. Dramatic engravings considered by many to be his greatest work. The terrifying space of the open sea, the storms and whirlpools of an unknown ocean, the ice of Antarctica, more—all rendered in a powerful, chilling manner. Full text. 38 plates. 77pp. 9¼ × 12. 22305-1 Pa. $4.95

THE EXPEDITIONS OF ZEBULON MONTGOMERY PIKE, Zebulon Montgomery Pike. Fascinating firsthand accounts (1805-6) of exploration of Mississippi River, Indian wars, capture by Spanish dragoons, much more. 1,088pp. 5⅜ × 8½. 25254-X, 25255-8 Pa., Two-vol. set $25.90

A CONCISE HISTORY OF PHOTOGRAPHY: Third Revised Edition, Helmut Gernsheim. Best one-volume history—camera obscura, photochemistry, daguerreotypes, evolution of cameras, film, more. Also artistic aspects—landscape, portraits, fine art, etc. 281 black-and-white photographs. 26 in color. 176pp. 8⅜ × 11¼.
25128-4 Pa. $14.95

THE DORÉ BIBLE ILLUSTRATIONS, Gustave Doré. 241 detailed plates from the Bible: the Creation scenes, Adam and Eve, Flood, Babylon, battle sequences, life of Jesus, etc. Each plate is accompanied by the verses from the King James version of the Bible. 241pp. 9 × 12.
23004-X Pa. $9.95

WANDERINGS IN WEST AFRICA, Richard F. Burton. Great Victorian scholar/ adventurer's invaluable descriptions of African tribal rituals, fetishism, culture, art, much more. Fascinating 19th-century account. 624pp. 5⅜ × 8½. 26890-X Pa. $12.95

FLATLAND, E. A. Abbott. Intriguing and enormously popular science-fiction classic explores the complexities of trying to survive as a two-dimensional being in a three-dimensional world. Amusingly illustrated by the author. 16 illustrations. 103pp. 5⅜ × 8½.
20001-9 Pa. $2.50

THE HISTORY OF THE LEWIS AND CLARK EXPEDITION, Meriwether Lewis and William Clark, edited by Elliott Coues. Classic edition of Lewis and Clark's day-by-day journals that later became the basis for U.S. claims to Oregon and the West. Accurate and invaluable geographical, botanical, biological, meteorological and anthropological material. Total of 1,508pp. 5⅜ × 8½.
21268-8, 21269-6, 21270-X Pa., Three-vol. set $29.85

LANGUAGE, TRUTH AND LOGIC, Alfred J. Ayer. Famous, clear introduction to Vienna, Cambridge schools of Logical Positivism. Role of philosophy, elimination of metaphysics, nature of analysis, etc. 160pp. 5⅜ × 8½. (Available in U.S. and Canada only)
20010-8 Pa. $3.95

MATHEMATICS FOR THE NONMATHEMATICIAN, Morris Kline. Detailed, college-level treatment of mathematics in cultural and historical context, with numerous exercises. For liberal arts students. Preface. Recommended Reading Lists. Tables. Index. Numerous black-and-white figures. xvi + 641pp. 5⅜ × 8½.
24823-2 Pa. $11.95

HANDBOOK OF PICTORIAL SYMBOLS, Rudolph Modley. 3,250 signs and symbols, many systems in full; official or heavy commercial use. Arranged by subject. Most in Pictorial Archive series. 143pp. 8¼ × 11. 23357-X Pa. $7.95

INCIDENTS OF TRAVEL IN YUCATAN, John L. Stephens. Classic (1843) exploration of jungles of Yucatan, looking for evidences of Maya civilization. Travel adventures, Mexican and Indian culture, etc. Total of 669pp. 5⅜ × 8½.
20926-1, 20927-X Pa., Two-vol. set $11.90

DEGAS: An Intimate Portrait, Ambroise Vollard. Charming, anecdotal memoir by famous art dealer of one of the greatest 19th-century French painters. 14 black-and-white illustrations. Introduction by Harold L. Van Doren. 96pp. 5⅜ × 8½.
25131-4 Pa. $4.95

PERSONAL NARRATIVE OF A PILGRIMAGE TO AL-MADINAH AND MECCAH, Richard F. Burton. Great travel classic by remarkably colorful personality. Burton, disguised as a Moroccan, visited sacred shrines of Islam, narrowly escaping death. 47 illustrations. 959pp. 5⅜ × 8½.
21217-3, 21218-1 Pa., Two-vol. set $19.90

PHRASE AND WORD ORIGINS, A. H. Holt. Entertaining, reliable, modern study of more than 1,200 colorful words, phrases, origins and histories. Much unexpected information. 254pp. 5⅜ × 8½.
20758-7 Pa. $5.95

THE RED THUMB MARK, R. Austin Freeman. In this first Dr. Thorndyke case, the great scientific detective draws fascinating conclusions from the nature of a single fingerprint. Exciting story, authentic science. 320pp. 5⅜ × 8½. (Available in U.S. only)
25210-8 Pa. $6.95

AN EGYPTIAN HIEROGLYPHIC DICTIONARY, E. A. Wallis Budge. Monumental work containing about 25,000 words or terms that occur in texts ranging from 3000 B.C. to 600 A.D. Each entry consists of a transliteration of the word, the word in hieroglyphs, and the meaning in English. 1,314pp. 6⅝ × 10.
23615-3, 23616-1 Pa., Two-vol. set $35.90

THE COMPLEAT STRATEGYST: Being a Primer on the Theory of Games of Strategy, J. D. Williams. Highly entertaining classic describes, with many illustrated examples, how to select best strategies in conflict situations. Prefaces. Appendices. xvi + 268pp. 5⅜ × 8½.
25101-2 Pa. $6.95

THE ROAD TO OZ, L. Frank Baum. Dorothy meets the Shaggy Man, little Button-Bright and the Rainbow's beautiful daughter in this delightful trip to the magical Land of Oz. 272pp. 5⅜ × 8.
25208-6 Pa. $5.95

POINT AND LINE TO PLANE, Wassily Kandinsky. Seminal exposition of role of point, line, other elements in nonobjective painting. Essential to understanding 20th-century art. 127 illustrations. 192pp. 6½ × 9¼.
23808-3 Pa. $5.95

LADY ANNA, Anthony Trollope. Moving chronicle of Countess Lovel's bitter struggle to win for herself and daughter Anna their rightful rank and fortune—perhaps at cost of sanity itself. 384pp. 5⅜ × 8½.
24669-8 Pa. $8.95

EGYPTIAN MAGIC, E. A. Wallis Budge. Sums up all that is known about magic in Ancient Egypt: the role of magic in controlling the gods, powerful amulets that warded off evil spirits, scarabs of immortality, use of wax images, formulas and spells, the secret name, much more. 253pp. 5⅜ × 8½.
22681-6 Pa. $4.50

THE DANCE OF SIVA, Ananda Coomaraswamy. Preeminent authority unfolds the vast metaphysic of India: the revelation of her art, conception of the universe, social organization, etc. 27 reproductions of art masterpieces. 192pp. 5⅜ × 8½.
24817-8 Pa. $6.95

CHRISTMAS CUSTOMS AND TRADITIONS, Clement A. Miles. Origin, evolution, significance of religious, secular practices. Caroling, gifts, yule logs, much more. Full, scholarly yet fascinating; non-sectarian. 400pp. 5⅜ × 8½.
23354-5 Pa. $6.95

THE HUMAN FIGURE IN MOTION, Eadweard Muybridge. More than 4,500 stopped-action photos, in action series, showing undraped men, women, children jumping, lying down, throwing, sitting, wrestling, carrying, etc. 390pp. 7⅞ × 10⅝.
20204-6 Cloth. $24.95

THE MAN WHO WAS THURSDAY, Gilbert Keith Chesterton. Witty, fast-paced novel about a club of anarchists in turn-of-the-century London. Brilliant social, religious, philosophical speculations. 128pp. 5⅜ × 8½.
25121-7 Pa. $3.95

A CÉZANNE SKETCHBOOK: Figures, Portraits, Landscapes and Still Lifes, Paul Cézanne. Great artist experiments with tonal effects, light, mass, other qualities in over 100 drawings. A revealing view of developing master painter, precursor of Cubism. 102 black-and-white illustrations. 144pp. 8¾ × 6⅜.
24790-2 Pa. $6.95

AN ENCYCLOPEDIA OF BATTLES: Accounts of Over 1,560 Battles from 1479 B.C. to the Present, David Eggenberger. Presents essential details of every major battle in recorded history, from the first battle of Megiddo in 1479 B.C. to Grenada in 1984. List of Battle Maps. New Appendix covering the years 1967-1984. Index. 99 illustrations. 544pp. 6½ × 9¼.
24913-1 Pa. $14.95

AN ETYMOLOGICAL DICTIONARY OF MODERN ENGLISH, Ernest Weekley. Richest, fullest work, by foremost British lexicographer. Detailed word histories. Inexhaustible. Total of 856pp. 6½ × 9¼.
21873-2, 21874-0 Pa., Two-vol. set $19.90

WEBSTER'S AMERICAN MILITARY BIOGRAPHIES, edited by Robert McHenry. Over 1,000 figures who shaped 3 centuries of American military history. Detailed biographies of Nathan Hale, Douglas MacArthur, Mary Hallaren, others. Chronologies of engagements, more. Introduction. Addenda. 1,033 entries in alphabetical order. xi + 548pp. 6½ × 9¼. (Available in U.S. only)
24758-9 Pa. $13.95

LIFE IN ANCIENT EGYPT, Adolf Erman. Detailed older account, with much not in more recent books: domestic life, religion, magic, medicine, commerce, and whatever else needed for complete picture. Many illustrations. 597pp. 5⅜ × 8½.
22632-8 Pa. $8.95

HISTORIC COSTUME IN PICTURES, Braun & Schneider. Over 1,450 costumed figures shown, covering a wide variety of peoples: kings, emperors, nobles, priests, servants, soldiers, scholars, townsfolk, peasants, merchants, courtiers, cavaliers, and more. 256pp. 8⅜ × 11¼.
23150-X Pa. $9.95

THE NOTEBOOKS OF LEONARDO DA VINCI, edited by J. P. Richter. Extracts from manuscripts reveal great genius; on painting, sculpture, anatomy, sciences, geography, etc. Both Italian and English. 186 ms. pages reproduced, plus 500 additional drawings, including studies for *Last Supper, Sforza* monument, etc. 860pp. 7⅞ × 10¾. (Available in U.S. only) 22572-0, 22573-9 Pa., Two-vol. set $31.90

THE ART NOUVEAU STYLE BOOK OF ALPHONSE MUCHA: All 72 Plates from "Documents Decoratifs" in Original Color, Alphonse Mucha. Rare copy-right-free design portfolio by high priest of Art Nouveau. Jewelry, wallpaper, stained glass, furniture, figure studies, plant and animal motifs, etc. Only complete one-volume edition. 80pp. 9⅜ × 12¼. 24044-4 Pa. $10.95

ANIMALS: 1,419 Copyright-Free Illustrations of Mammals, Birds, Fish, Insects, Etc., edited by Jim Harter. Clear wood engravings present, in extremely lifelike poses, over 1,000 species of animals. One of the most extensive pictorial source-books of its kind. Captions. Index. 284pp. 9 × 12. 23766-4 Pa. $10.95

OBELISTS FLY HIGH, C. Daly King. Masterpiece of American detective fiction, long out of print, involves murder on a 1935 transcontinental flight—"a very thrilling story"—NY Times. Unabridged and unaltered republication of the edition published by William Collins Sons & Co. Ltd., London, 1935. 288pp. 5⅜ × 8½. (Available in U.S. only) 25036-9 Pa. $5.95

VICTORIAN AND EDWARDIAN FASHION: A Photographic Survey, Alison Gernsheim. First fashion history completely illustrated by contemporary photo-graphs. Full text plus 235 photos, 1840-1914, in which many celebrities appear. 240pp. 6½ × 9¼. 24205-6 Pa. $8.95

THE ART OF THE FRENCH ILLUSTRATED BOOK, 1700-1914, Gordon N. Ray. Over 630 superb book illustrations by Fragonard, Delacroix, Daumier, Doré, Grandville, Manet, Mucha, Steinlen, Toulouse-Lautrec and many others. Preface. Introduction. 633 halftones. Indices of artists, authors & titles, binders and provenances. Appendices. Bibliography. 608pp. 8⅜ × 11¼. 25086-5 Pa. $24.95

THE WONDERFUL WIZARD OF OZ, L. Frank Baum. Facsimile in full color of America's finest children's classic. 143 illustrations by W. W. Denslow. 267pp. 5⅜ × 8½. 20691-2 Pa. $7.95

FOLLOWING THE EQUATOR: A Journey Around the World, Mark Twain. Great writer's 1897 account of circumnavigating the globe by steamship. Ironic humor, keen observations, vivid and fascinating descriptions of exotic places. 197 illustrations. 720pp. 5⅜ × 8½. 26113-1 Pa. $15.95

THE FRIENDLY STARS, Martha Evans Martin & Donald Howard Menzel. Classic text marshalls the stars together in an engaging, nontechnical survey, presenting them as sources of beauty in night sky. 23 illustrations. Foreword. 2 star charts. Index. 147pp. 5⅜ × 8½. 21099-5 Pa. $3.95

FADS AND FALLACIES IN THE NAME OF SCIENCE, Martin Gardner. Fair, witty appraisal of cranks, quacks, and quackeries of science and pseudoscience: hollow earth, Velikovsky, orgone energy, Dianetics, flying saucers, Bridey Murphy, food and medical fads, etc. Revised, expanded In the Name of Science. "A very able and even-tempered presentation."—The New Yorker. 363pp. 5⅜ × 8. 20394-8 Pa. $6.95

ANCIENT EGYPT: Its Culture and History, J. E. Manchip White. From pre-dynastics through Ptolemies: society, history, political structure, religion, daily life, literature, cultural heritage. 48 plates. 217pp. 5⅜ × 8½. 22548-8 Pa. $5.95

SIR HARRY HOTSPUR OF HUMBLETHWAITE, Anthony Trollope. Incisive, unconventional psychological study of a conflict between a wealthy baronet, his idealistic daughter, and their scapegrace cousin. The 1870 novel in its first inexpensive edition in years. 250pp. 5⅜ × 8½. 24953-0 Pa. $6.95

LASERS AND HOLOGRAPHY, Winston E. Kock. Sound introduction to burgeoning field, expanded (1981) for second edition. Wave patterns, coherence, lasers, diffraction, zone plates, properties of holograms, recent advances. 84 illustrations. 160pp. 5⅜ × 8¼. (Except in United Kingdom) 24041-X Pa. $3.95

INTRODUCTION TO ARTIFICIAL INTELLIGENCE: Second, Enlarged Edition, Philip C. Jackson, Jr. Comprehensive survey of artificial intelligence—the study of how machines (computers) can be made to act intelligently. Includes introductory and advanced material. Extensive notes updating the main text. 132 black-and-white illustrations. 512pp. 5⅜ × 8½. 24864-X Pa. $10.95

HISTORY OF INDIAN AND INDONESIAN ART, Ananda K. Coomaraswamy. Over 400 illustrations illuminate classic study of Indian art from earliest Harappa finds to early 20th century. Provides philosophical, religious and social insights. 304pp. 6⅝ × 9⅜. 25005-9 Pa. $11.95

THE GOLEM, Gustav Meyrink. Most famous supernatural novel in modern European literature, set in Ghetto of Old Prague around 1890. Compelling story of mystical experiences, strange transformations, profound terror. 13 black-and-white illustrations. 224pp. 5⅜ × 8½. (Available in U.S. only) 25025-3 Pa. $6.95

PICTORIAL ENCYCLOPEDIA OF HISTORIC ARCHITECTURAL PLANS, DETAILS AND ELEMENTS: With 1,880 Line Drawings of Arches, Domes, Doorways, Facades, Gables, Windows, etc., John Theodore Haneman. Sourcebook of inspiration for architects, designers, others. Bibliography. Captions. 141pp. 9 × 12. 24605-1 Pa. $7.95

BENCHLEY LOST AND FOUND, Robert Benchley. Finest humor from early 30s, about pet peeves, child psychologists, post office and others. Mostly unavailable elsewhere. 73 illustrations by Peter Arno and others. 183pp. 5⅜ × 8½. 22410-4 Pa. $4.95

ERTÉ GRAPHICS, Erté. Collection of striking color graphics: Seasons, Alphabet, Numerals, Aces and Precious Stones. 50 plates, including 4 on covers. 48pp. 9⅜ × 12¼. 23580-7 Pa. $7.95

THE JOURNAL OF HENRY D. THOREAU, edited by Bradford Torrey, F. H. Allen. Complete reprinting of 14 volumes, 1837–61, over two million words; the sourcebooks for Walden, etc. Definitive. All original sketches, plus 75 photographs. 1,804pp. 8½ × 12¼. 20312-3, 20313-1 Cloth., Two-vol. set $130.00

CASTLES: Their Construction and History, Sidney Toy. Traces castle development from ancient roots. Nearly 200 photographs and drawings illustrate moats, keeps, baileys, many other features. Caernarvon, Dover Castles, Hadrian's Wall, Tower of London, dozens more. 256pp. 5⅜ × 8¼. 24898-4 Pa. $6.95

CATALOG OF DOVER BOOKS

AMERICAN CLIPPER SHIPS: 1833–1858, Octavius T. Howe & Frederick C. Matthews. Fully-illustrated, encyclopedic review of 352 clipper ships from the period of America's greatest maritime supremacy. Introduction. 109 halftones. 5 black-and-white line illustrations. Index. Total of 928pp. 5⅜ × 8½.
25115-2, 25116-0 Pa., Two-vol. set $17.90

TOWARDS A NEW ARCHITECTURE, Le Corbusier. Pioneering manifesto by great architect, near legendary founder of "International School." Technical and aesthetic theories, views on industry, economics, relation of form to function, "mass-production spirit," much more. Profusely illustrated. Unabridged translation of 13th French edition. Introduction by Frederick Etchells. 320pp. 6⅛ × 9¼. (Available in U.S. only)
25023-7 Pa. $8.95

THE BOOK OF KELLS, edited by Blanche Cirker. Inexpensive collection of 32 full-color, full-page plates from the greatest illuminated manuscript of the Middle Ages, painstakingly reproduced from rare facsimile edition. Publisher's Note. Captions. 32pp. 9⅜ × 12¼.
24345-1 Pa. $5.95

BEST SCIENCE FICTION STORIES OF H. G. WELLS, H. G. Wells. Full novel *The Invisible Man*, plus 17 short stories: "The Crystal Egg," "Aepyornis Island," "The Strange Orchid," etc. 303pp. 5⅜ × 8½. (Available in U.S. only)
21531-8 Pa. $6.95

AMERICAN SAILING SHIPS: Their Plans and History, Charles G. Davis. Photos, construction details of schooners, frigates, clippers, other sailcraft of 18th to early 20th centuries—plus entertaining discourse on design, rigging, nautical lore, much more. 137 black-and-white illustrations. 240pp. 6⅛ × 9¼.
24658-2 Pa. $6.95

ENTERTAINING MATHEMATICAL PUZZLES, Martin Gardner. Selection of author's favorite conundrums involving arithmetic, money, speed, etc., with lively commentary. Complete solutions. 112pp. 5⅜ × 8½.
25211-6 Pa. $3.50

THE WILL TO BELIEVE, HUMAN IMMORTALITY, William James. Two books bound together. Effect of irrational on logical, and arguments for human immortality. 402pp. 5⅜ × 8½.
20291-7 Pa. $8.95

THE HAUNTED MONASTERY and THE CHINESE MAZE MURDERS, Robert Van Gulik. 2 full novels by Van Gulik continue adventures of Judge Dee and his companions. An evil Taoist monastery, seemingly supernatural events; overgrown topiary maze that hides strange crimes. Set in 7th-century China. 27 illustrations. 328pp. 5⅜ × 8½.
23502-5 Pa. $6.95

CELEBRATED CASES OF JUDGE DEE (DEE GOONG AN), translated by Robert Van Gulik. Authentic 18th-century Chinese detective novel; Dee and associates solve three interlocked cases. Led to Van Gulik's own stories with same characters. Extensive introduction. 9 illustrations. 237pp. 5⅜ × 8½.
23337-5 Pa. $5.95

Prices subject to change without notice.

Available at your book dealer or write for free catalog to Dept. GI, Dover Publications, Inc., 31 East 2nd St., Mineola, N.Y. 11501. Dover publishes more than 175 books each year on science, elementary and advanced mathematics, biology, music, art, literary history, social sciences and other areas.